DO YOUR OWN P.R.

Getting the right publicity for your organisation

Ian Phillipson

How To Books

Other books by the same author

How to Start Word Processing
How to Work from Home

British Library Cataloguing in Publication Data
A catalogue record for this book is available from the British Library.

© Copyright 1995 by Ian Phillipson

First published in 1995 by How To Books Ltd, Plymbridge House,
Estover Road, Plymouth PL6 7PZ, United Kingdom. Tel: (01752) 735251/
695745. Fax: (01752) 695699. Telex: 45635.

Note: The material contained in this book is set out in good faith for general
guidance and no liability can be accepted for loss or expense incurred as a result
of relying in particular circumstances on statements made in the book. The laws
and regulations are complex and liable to change, and readers should check the
current position with the relevant authorities before making personal
arrangements.

Typeset by PDQ Typesetting, Stoke-on-Trent, Staffs.
Printed and bound by The Cromwell Press Ltd, Broughton Gifford, Melksham,
Wiltshire.

HOW TO DO YOUR OWN P.R.

72

In this Series

Other titles in preparation

Contents

List of Illustrations

Preface

Oddly enough for a profession whose main aim is to promote and portray others in the best light, public relations itself has rather a bad image. It's seen as being manipulative, underhand, dishonest and the preserve of corrupt big business and roguish politicians.

I hope this book will go some little way to put an opposite view, and show how you can use PR profitably, easily and ethically whether you are a business, voluntary group, charity, school or individual.

By the end of *How to Do Your Own PR* you should have a good understanding of public relations, not as an academic subject but as a valuable and highly practical tool of use to anyone who wants to present themselves in the best possible light.

The ideas and techniques you'll find within these pages won't be applicable to everyone, so think of this book as providing a menu of possibilities to be picked at as best fits your own particular budget, time and circumstances.

So, good luck with your reading and my thanks to all those small businesses I have been fortunate enough to be associated with in my years as a public relations and publicity consultant.

Ian Phillipson

IS THIS YOU?

Club secretary   Business person

                              Manager

Librarian   Would-be entrepreneur

                              Author

Designer   Student

                              Teacher

School governor   Accountant

                              Artist

Alternative health practitioner   Local councillor

                        Charity worker

Committee member   Action group member

                            Fundraiser

Market researcher   Solicitor

                      Trade union official

Event organiser   Curator

                          Sales person

Publisher   Trainer

                    Management consultant

Actor   Gym owner

                            Performer

Estate agent   Journalist

                          Church worker

Travel agent   Hotelier

                              Advisor

Counsellor   Insurance broker

                          Antique dealer

Financial consultant   Publican

                            Jobseeker

Book keeper   College staff

                      Garden centre owner

Local authority manager   Interior designer

                    Tourist attraction owner

Franchisee   Theatre manager

1
Public Relations and You

'The meek shall inherit the Earth, but they'll never increase their market share.' William G McGowan.

'There is only one thing in the world worse than being talked about, and that's not being talked about.' Oscar Wilde, *The Picture of Dorian Gray*.

WHAT IS PR?

'A man takes a girl out for a romantic evening. At the end of it he tells her that he's the world's best lover – that's advertising. If he tells her she needs a lover and he's the best man for the job – that's marketing. But if, before he can say a word she tells him that she's heard he's a great lover – then that's public relations.'

Forget academic definitions, public relations, or PR, largely entails trying to make sure a favourable message about you is projected to the right people at the right time. That's something nearly every business small or large, every association, event, pressure group, ambitious individual, voluntary body or non-profit making institution would surely like to try to do!

Public relations can help you do many things such as

- develop a corporate identity and image

- create goodwill amongst customers, suppliers or the local community

- promote and raise awareness of yourself or company

- obtain favourable press coverage

- help you become more accepted in the local community

- change the way people think about you.

11

The vehicles of PR

The majority of PR work is done through the media, that is newspapers, magazines, radio and television. To a lesser extent public speaking and company newsletters also have their part. We will look at all of these in turn, their advantages and disadvantages and consider how you can exploit them to the full.

What PR can and cannot do

Though it's an invaluable tool PR does have limitations and it's important to understand what these are, if you are to appreciate when some other form of promotion should be undertaken.

1. First, because you don't pay the media, or anyone else, to give you PR coverage there is no guarantee that you will ever get any, or that your PR story will ever appear at a particular time or in a particular publication. Of course, you can do your best to make sure this happens, and this book will show you how to do that, but there's no certainty at all. This is unlike advertising in which you pay for a certain size of space in a certain publication on a certain day. Every PR consultant knows of the story that never appeared because it was sent out on the very day that a disaster or political scandal broke.

2. Second, neither is there any guarantee that your PR message or story will appear in exactly the way that you want it to. You can supply your story, but then it will be left to others, journalists and editors, to determine how it will actually appear.

3. And third, your PR story will only rate the space it warrants. So, if you run a small pet shop you'll find it far harder to put yourself in the news than if you're a multinational company employing thousands of people and with far greater resources. For one thing you just aren't going to have enough happening to generate great numbers of news stories, and for another you won't have the time or the finances to continually feed your name to the press.

Can you do it?

For the most part doing your own PR isn't difficult, though more complicated activity may require additional and even expert help. All it takes is some thought, a modicum of writing skill, a degree of confidence and organisational ability and you're there.

You certainly aren't disadvantaged by not being a professional PR person. The press will talk to anybody. In some cases you will even

A telephone

This is an absolute must. You'll need to give a phone contact number when sending out information. Once more there's no need for fancy equipment, though a phone with a memory for twenty or so numbers saves time leafing through the phone book.

When you're in full promotional flow a **mobile phone** can help journalists reach you, wherever you are. This is very important in the later stages of organising an event, or when you have just issued a press release, but can't stay in the one place to answer enquiries. Give your mobile as the main number on press releases if this is likely to be the case. If you don't want the expense of a mobile phone, then a **bleeper** is the cost effective alternative.

A fax

A fax machine is perhaps not essential, but it is almost so since it allows you to issue press releases very quickly to meet the imminent deadlines of newspapers. Editorial offices don't seem to mind releases being sent in this way, though don't abuse their usefulness by sending out non-urgent releases that could have gone by mail. One potential problem with faxes is that you have no guarantee it will end up where you think it will, or that it won't be picked up by the wrong person. Remember this if you're sending confidential information.

Stationery

Though your standard letterheads can be used for promotional work, specially designed and printed Press Release paper is better since it is less likely to be confused with a standard letter and lost or overlooked on a cluttered desk. If you are in business make sure the paper is good quality as your image is important. If you are a charity or non-profit making organisation then consider using recycled paper, which helps establish your credibility as a 'caring' organisation.

PRESS RELEASE should be printed on the paper either horizontally at the top of the page or vertically down the side. This can be done in colour or just in black and white, as your budget allows.

Case history

Since her department had no budget for properly printed release paper Janice used standard letterheads with PRESS RELEASE printed along the top to promote events for the local council. But not satisfied with this, Janice began adding illustrations to the paper to give it more character and to make the release easier to identify on a desk full of paper. Adding the illustration was easy enough. She just

Press Release

HOCKEY JOCKEYS
RIDE INTO TOWN

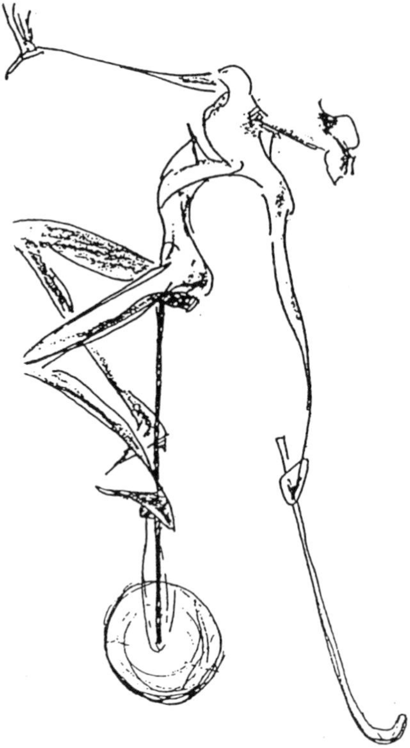

Unicycle hockey wobbles into Worcestershire 26 September 199X, when teams from all over the south of England compete at the Girl's College, Malvern (noon start).

Played between two teams of five competing over 30 minutes, unicycle hockey is fast and furious with much skill... and spills. Just try and hit a ball with a hockey stick when sitting on a bike with one wheel! GREAT PICTURE POTENTIAL.

Teams from as far as Sussex, London and Bristol will be competing with the winners being presented with a striking three-foot-high fibreglass trophy of a unicycle hockey player, created by artist Sarah Watson.

The tournament is one of the last events in Malvern's Victorian Celebrations, 23-26 September 199X.

13 September 199X

For further information contact: Ian Phillipson, Ideas that Sell Publicity (01886) 880532.

Fig. 2. An illustrated press release.

took an appropriate image from a book and photocopied it. She then stuck the photocopied image onto a master copy, using the reducing and enlarging facility to create the right size of illustration. She then photocopied this onto other sheets. If the illustration had a peculiar shape then she just flowed the text of the release around it using a word processor.

Copyright problems

Though unlikely to be taken to court for breach of copyright you should be aware that **copyright** does apply to any illustrations you might copy. To cover yourself, ask for written permission from the owners of the illustration. You may have to pay a small fee for usage. Alternatively, ask an artist (or art student) to create an image for you. The stylized unicycle hockey player was created this way.

Standard business envelopes are adequate for most purposes. Again charities might benefit from using recycled envelopes. Use

- DL for sending out two or three A4 sheets folded twice

- C5 for three to five A4 sheets folded once

- C4 when sending out six or more unfolded A4 sheets.

If photographs are to accompany press releases send everything out in card backed envelopes which are overprinted with 'Please Do Not Bend'.

A camera

If you intend taking your own PR photographs a 35 mm SLR (single lens reflex) camera will cope with most you can throw at it, though for head and shoulder snapshots, a good quality idiot-proof camera is generally sufficient. You'll need different speeds of film for different lighting conditions.

A tape recorder

A hand held machine will not only let you record conversations with journalists but is also a good means of putting down ideas when they come to you in a burst of creativity. Microphones are available which can be stuck on the receiver to record phone interviews. It is perfectly legal to record a phone conversation to which you are party; you do not have to tell the other person that you are recording. Only if recording a third party's call do you need to do that.

EQUIPPING YOURSELF WITH INFORMATION

Keeping a contact book

You will need some system for keeping names and addresses of journalists, media contacts, photographers, designers and other sub-contractors. The simplest method is to use an A4 sized index book with narrow ruled pages. This will give you space to also make a few notes about your contact, their likes, dislikes, enthusiasms and specialities. Alternatively use index cards, one for each contact. These can either be stored in boxes, or better still on a swivel file, such as a Roladex. Those more technologically minded will want to store the information on computer. This is fast and has the added advantage of being able to generate address labels for mailouts. But remember, if you keep personal information on computer, you may need to register under the Data Protection Act. If you keep your contact list on computer, periodically make a hard copy.

Directories and information sources

Unless you are already involved in publishing or public relations, you probably just won't be aware of how many publications there are on the market. The newspapers and magazines (all potential homes for your PR stories) you see in even the largest newsagents are just the tip of an absolutely massive iceberg.

To find out just what publications are available you'll find a number of specialist directories particularly useful. In no particular order of preference these include:

- *Willings Press Guide*. A two-volume listing of magazines and newspapers in the UK and overseas. Published annually.

- *Writers' and Artists' Yearbook*. Listings of newspapers and magazines and their editors, along with brief information on their editorial requirements. An annual publication.

- *The Writer's Handbook*. Similar to the *Writers' and Artists' Yearbook*. Again published annually.

- *Benn's Media Directory*. Two-volume listing of newspapers and magazines covering both the UK and overseas. Updated once a year.

- *PIMS UK Media Directory*. Divided by category, this lists national and regional newspapers, their editors and special correspondents.

Contacts are also given for radio and TV feature programmes. There is also freelance journalist section. Updated monthly.

- *PR Planner.* A two-volume directory (UK and Europe). Similar to *PIMS.*

- *BRAD (British Rate and Data).* Though primarily for advertisers *BRAD* covers most British publications. It gives circulation, editors and key staff as well as advertising information. Updated monthly.

- *Editors.* In six volumes this provides the most comprehensive listing of journalists and UK publications.

- *ADVANCE Editorial Features Director* provides details of special editorial features planned for the UK Press. Expensive at £225 but highly useful.

You are likely to find *The Writer's Handbook, The Writers' and Artists' Yearbook, BRAD, Willings* and *Benn's Media Directory* in most libraries with a decent reference section, but *Editors, PR Planner* and *PIMS* are more specialist publications and not so readily available.

Your information action plan
Draw up a list of all local newspapers and magazines, radio and television stations. Add to these any specialist magazines and trade journals in which you would like to appear. Do that here:

....

....

....

....

....

....

Start developing your news sense by looking through the papers. Try to spot which might be 'placed' PR stories and which might 'be news' that a reporter has been brought or stumbled upon. After a while you will begin to see that some publications seem to 'specialise' in certain types of news, while tackling the same story in different ways

POINTS FOR DISCUSSION

1. What would be the most essential items of equipment you would need for your own PR work, and which would you need to obtain first?

2. Which is the biggest reference library which you could get to easily from your workplace?

3. What specialised sources of contacts might you need?

3
Creating a Story to Sell

WHAT IS NEWS?

Though it may often seem otherwise, the media (newspapers, magazines, radio and television) aren't just interested in big bad things, they want a regular flow of information about the smaller good news, too, and you can help provide them with that in a variety of forms.

You only have to look through three or four different newspapers to see how differently daily life is treated in all its glory and to see that one person's news is not necessarily another's. While the tabloids like to focus on the triumphs and disasters of human life in all its infinite variety and detail, the heavies go in for the hard news: the things that we all 'ought' to be interested in, such as politics, war and commerce.

But whatever the story, it still needs to meet some basic news criteria, if not all of those listed below, then at least many of them in some mix or another depending entirely in which newspaper or publication they appear.

Six news criteria
1. Relevance
It has to be considered relevant so people will be interested in it. It's a waste of time sending a story on peculiar pigs to *Rambling Today* magazine, enthralling though your tale of Bertha the window cleaning porker may be, it just won't grip them.

2. Newsworthiness
It has to be newsworthy. While some events are newsworthy whatever the circumstance – for instance so called 'hard news' such as general elections, tragedies and coronations – the newsworthiness of most stories ebbs and flows. And though newsworthy stories are generally new, they don't have to be. Old news is frequently recycled if it hasn't appeared in the press for several years.

3. Topicality

It has to be topical. News grows old very quickly, though at different speeds. Financial news can be old hat in a matter of moments, while information about a new paint has a longer shelf life. One thing is sure however; the older it is the less newsworthy something becomes.

4. Human interest

It should preferably contain a human interest factor. Your story should relate to people, so someone should be either at the centre of the story, or the story must in some way affect people.

5. The element of conflict

Your story should contain some degree of conflict. Conflict doesn't have to involve a war, a battle or even a minor scuffle; it just means that there must be some difficulty or barrier which makes it harder for something to happen.

For instance, you have news when something goes against you, say if planning permission is turned down for a new factory, or premises. This could give you a whole number of possible conflict stories such as:

- the local council isn't doing its best for business, just at a time when the town could do with a new boost to the economy;

- the planning department is corrupt (you'd better be sure of your facts before taking this line, if you don't want to be sued);

- or you'll have to relocate elsewhere taking jobs with you from the town.

6. Originality

Ideally the story should have some originality. This doesn't mean that it's a story no one has ever seen before. An original story can be a story that has appeared before, but this time with a new slant.

7. Different

News should be different in some way. If you put out the same story as everyone else, then why should your story be used in preference to theirs?

Example: Joanna seizes her chance

One of the features of a good story is that it should contain an element of human interest, but human interest can also mean animal interest, as Joanna who runs a rather exclusive ladies' clothes shop exploited to the full.

One day, shortly after she'd opened, the cat from the pub next door wandered inside and jumped into the front window. Rather than throw him out, Joanna – something of a self confessed 'softy' – let the cat stay and was glad she had. Very soon passersby began stopping in front of the shop to peer in at the furry window decoration, by now contentedly sleeping his head off. Inevitably some of those passing by came into the shop. Indeed, one woman said that if she hadn't spotted the cat, she'd never have seen the hat she wanted for a wedding.

Seizing upon the chance, Joanna phoned up the editor of the local paper who, amused by the story, sent along a photographer. Again, more useful news coverage, with Joanna's establishment soon becoming 'the shop with the cat'.

All this happened by accident but that doesn't matter, Joanna grabbed the PR opportunity when it presented itself. But you could create a similar opportunity for yourself.

HOW TO DEVELOP AN ANGLE

While there are certain events and circumstances that are genuinely newsworthy to the press, 'non-news events' can suddenly become interesting to the press if they are given an angle. An angle is a way of looking at a news story that makes it right for one publication and not another.

Indeed, it would not be exaggerating to suggest that over 50 per cent of the stories in national newspapers are PR stories, that have simply been given an eye-catching angle!

This may sound false, Machiavellian almost, and if it does then you'll just have to wait until what you feel is a 'genuine' story comes along for you to publicise. However, there seems nothing wrong in looking at a story from all directions just to see how it can be presented in the best light.

Action tip

Practise seeing different angles in news stories that you read in the local and national press. Take any of today's daily newspapers, choose a news story and try to see how many news angles you could get from it by focusing on different aspects of the story.

*The story*_____

*Angle 1*_____

*Angle 2*_____

*Angle 3*_____

Example

Adrian runs a small ice cream production factory. On the hottest day of the year he approaches a local engineering company and offers to give all of its hot and bothered staff an ice cream each. Knowing that there is a press opportunity here, the firm agrees. The press are called and the next week a picture of the smiling workers and Adrian appears in the local press. A nice piece of publicity before a summer heatwave.

With this kind of thinking if Adrian had been a glove manufacturer he would have found a company with cold-fingered workers and donated so many pairs.

YOUR STORY-FINDING CHECKLISTS

Many organisations and businesses new to public relations have great difficulty in identifying news. But news and story ideas are all around. The following checklist should help you identify some possible stories.

Checklist 1

Has anyone in your organisation:

- unusual academic qualifications?
- unusual hobbies?
- an unusual talent?
- unusual work experience or background?
- won awards?
- particular sporting talents?
- unusual interests?
- achieved recognition for something they've done?
- worked with somebody famous?
- a particular area of expertise?

Checklist 2

Do you:

- have someone very young or old working for you?
- send staff on unusual courses?
- use odd materials in manufacturing?
- supply an unusual market?
- have unusual suppliers?
- have staff who work funny hours?
- have someone retiring who has an unusual story to tell?
- have any newsworthy people in your company?

Checklist 3

Are you:

- appointing someone new to your staff?
- taking on more staff?
- having difficulty recruiting staff?
- being visited by someone important?
- returning to traditional working methods?
- involving animals in your work?
- the first to do something in the area, or nationally?
- participating in an unusual sponsorship scheme?
- the first tenant in a new building?
- the last tenant in an old building?

Checklist 4

Has your organisation:

- changed the way it works, perhaps adding more shifts?
- been awarded a large contract?
- solved a major crisis?
- been able to improve a product?
- launched a new product?
- started selling in a different or unusual way?
- opened up an export market?
- found a new use for a product?
- changed its policies?
- an interesting event coming up?
- an anniversary coming up?
- arranged a stunt or strange event?
- done something worthwhile in the community?
- a strange incentive scheme?
- expansion plans?
- solved a customer or client problem particularly effectively?
- found something unusual at the premises during renovation?

Checklist 5

Are your premises:

- haunted by a ghost?
- particularly old?
- particularly unusual or different?

Checklist 6
Have you:

* rescued a failing business?
* bought another company?
* just hit a milestone (making your millionth widget)?

Action

The above are just a few of the questions you can ask about your organisation. Try adding to this list with your own questions.

Think back over the last twelve months and identify stories about your business or organisation that would have been of interest to the press. If you don't think the stories were quite as strong as you would have liked, then think of ways in which you could have spiced them up and given them some 'topspin'. List the stories here:

1. ....

2. ....

3. ....

4. ....

5. ....

Begin practising your newly acquired PR skills before you really need to use them. If a story does arise, then Murphy's Law says it will occur just when you are at your busiest and most pressurised. Don't leave it until then.

HOW TO IMPROVE YOUR CREATIVITY

'Discovery consists of looking at the same thing as everyone else and thinking something different,' concluded Albert Szent Gyorgyi, Nobel Prize-winning physicist. And since public relations requires a modicum of imagination to squeeze the pips from a story, learning to generate ideas on a regular basis is a skill worth acquiring. The following exercises, if performed regularly, will help you do that.

Brainstorming

Set up brainstorming sessions with other members of your business or organisation, or even friends or relatives. The idea is to have a free ranging session with as many ideas generated as possible, no matter how silly they may seem. Don't be critical of them during the session, leave the analysis until later otherwise you will get bogged down and lose the creativity, or people will be reluctant to speak if they think they will be criticised. Remember a good idea is a good idea irrespective of its source. And don't worry about having to come up with blindingly original ideas the whole time. Generally even the most original ideas are merely adaptations of old ones.

Setting up an ideas file

Hunt and scavenge everywhere for ideas that can be used for your PR and adapt them to your needs. While there is no ownership of a good idea, never blatantly copy an idea off a local rival as this will hardly set you apart from them.

Think positively

Take every opportunity to be creative. It doesn't matter in what sphere you do this. And start thinking of yourself as a creative person. You can come up with good ideas, so don't tell yourself you can't.

CHECKLIST – DO YOU HAVE A STORY?

	Yes	No
• Is your story idea topical?	____	____
• Is there something that is happening locally, regionally or nationally that can act as a peg on which you can hang your story?	____	____
• Is the story relevant to the people who will read it?	____	____
• Is the story different in some way? Does the story have a freshness about it? Remember old stories can be recycled.	____	____
• Is the story original?	____	____

NATIONAL OR LOCAL COVERAGE?

For a small business, the main PR vehicle will be the local newspaper and radio, so is there any point trying for national coverage? Well, yes, there is. Though of course the dailies will have less interest in putting local details into their stories an appearance in their pages makes your story somehow more legitimate and of interest locally because you are something of a celebrity (isn't anyone or anything that appears in the national press?); second, cuttings are cuttings and one from the *Daily Telegraph* or *The Times* can add to your credibility if you use it for promotional purposes; and third, if you've appeared in the national press the story should be picked up by the locals, even if it's been passed over previously by them. How can they ignore a 'national' story right on their doorstep?

Case history: Douglas's estate agency

Douglas runs an estate agency in a small country town. He's been in business for the last fifteen years and knows the area well. Like all those in the property market things have not gone too well over the last few years, but there are now signs that things are beginning to pick up. House prices have certainly stabilised and are even showing signs they might actually be going up. That's why Douglas is horrified to read a report in the Sunday papers on a survey by one of the larger building societies which says that prices are still dropping. This is not going to do his clients' confidence any good at all.

So, that afternoon Douglas drafts out a press release which states that prices locally are not falling and that he has records to prove it. He also has a dig at national organisations thinking they know about conditions locally, providing a good spicy quote. This he fires off on the Monday morning to the local press. The result: his remarks are covered in several publications and he gets a radio interview for a local station out of it. Douglas's annoyance with the national organisation is a key element in arousing local interest and sympathy.

Action tip

Even if you run the smallest of local businesses or organisations, constantly look through the national press for good news stories that you can develop at a local or regional level.

POINTS FOR DISCUSSION

1. What help could you get from your work colleagues in creating PR ideas for your organisation?

2. Of the various PR ideas you could develop, which is the most newsworthy right now?

3. Look through your local newspaper. Which of the news items do you think were prompted by PR activity?

4
How to Write a Press Release

'For there is good news yet to hear and fine things to be seen.'
G. K. Chesterton.

'When a dog bites a man that is not news, but when a man bites a dog that is news.' Charles Anderson Dana in the *New York Sun*, 1882.

WHAT IS A PRESS RELEASE?

The press release is the workhorse of the PR business so consequently journalists receive sackfuls of them – most of them second rate. Therefore it's hardly surprising that they tend to be looked at only briefly and end up in the bin. This means that every release you send out is up against it. This chapter should help you improve the chances of success.

When to use a press release
Press releases should be sent out only when you have something newsworthy to say. If you haven't then don't bother because your efforts will be ineffective and end up in the wastepaper bin and costing you money in time, postage and materials.

Press releases are likely to be used when launching a new product, moving premises, expanding, countering rumours, announcing business successes and new events, just to name a few of the occasions.

GRABBING ATTENTION

Many forms of writing are intended to keep the reader in suspense until the end, not so with the press release. Indeed the very opposite is true since it's the function of a press release to give the game away about its content immediately.

Writing a headline
Every press release should begin with a headline. If you can write a witty one that will make the journalist smile it will increase the

chances that the release is read. But don't expect your headline to be used, sub-editors take pride in writing their own. However, if you can't think of an eye catching one, don't worry, very few journalists or editors are going to reject out of hand a good news story because it has a bad headline.

Witty or not, the headline should encapsulate the story, be simple to understand and free from jargon. And take care when choosing a writing style for the headline. Don't come up with a headline that is suitable for the tabloid papers and then send it to the quality broadsheets.

Writing the first paragraph

More important than the headline is the opening paragraph to your release, which should be as much like the lead paragraph of a newspaper story as possible. This means it should contain all information necessary to give a basic understanding of the story immediately.

It should say

WHAT the story is about

WHO the story involves or concerns

WHEN the story is taking (or took) place

WHY it is taking place at all

HOW it is taking place and

WHERE it is taking place.

Example
For instance:
Anytown's (where) Grosvenor Hall (who) will close (what) on Friday, 13 March 199X (when), unless £5000 can be found to keep it open (why).

This opening makes a dramatic statement (that the hall will close), which has a shock effect on many who probably didn't even know that it was in trouble. The 'unless', which delivers an element of uncertainty, is hidden in the body of the sentence.

The above is very much a standard leading paragraph with which to open a press release, but there are other ways. You can have:

- **a quotation lead** –
'By the year 2,001, 10 million people will be working from home', forecasts homeworking expert Ian Phillipson;

- a **question lead** –
  Will Britain be a nation of homeworkers by the year 2,001? One leading UK expert claims that it will be;

- or a **humorous lead** –
  Who doesn't go out to work, can stay in bed until they want and will number 10 million by the year 2,001? Britain's homeworkers, that's who!

The humorous lead is a riskier start because if the journalist who reads it doesn't share your sense of humour then your release may fall on barren ground. But if the story warrants this line the humorous lead can make a memorable impression.

WRITING THE BODY COPY

Be factual

Subsequent paragraphs of a press release merely expand and give extra detail about what has already been said. Like the lead paragraph they need to be written in a factual manner. A press release is not the place to be self-indulgent or self-congratulatory.

However, don't be afraid to quote yourself (or others from your organisation) in the release. If you do this you may like to provide another contact name at the bottom. When the press ring up, that person can then pass the call directly on to you. This helps suggest slightly less self interest on your part. It is only a small cosmetic change, but every little helps.

Don't get basic facts wrong. If you do, and a journalist knows or discovers this, then they'll wonder what else about your story is incorrect or misleading. This applies to all your PR activity.

Avoid clichés

Likewise, avoid writing in clichés. You will obscure your message and make the release read like so many other second-raters. If you make an assertion or statement in the release, especially if it is controversial, then try to back it up with a supportive comment or quote from an authority, or at least a named individual.

Tailor the content

Tailor the wording and structure of your press release to increase the interest to particular publications, remember to give it that slant. This could mean altering the headline, emphasising one aspect of the story and not another, or adding an additional sentence.

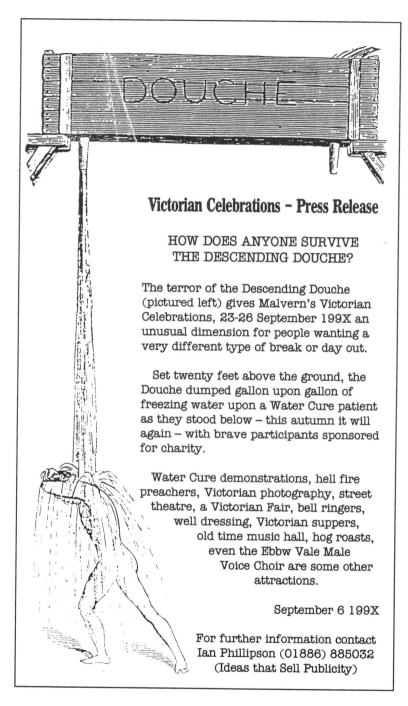

Victorian Celebrations - Press Release

HOW DOES ANYONE SURVIVE THE DESCENDING DOUCHE?

The terror of the Descending Douche (pictured left) gives Malvern's Victorian Celebrations, 23-26 September 199X an unusual dimension for people wanting a very different type of break or day out.

Set twenty feet above the ground, the Douche dumped gallon upon gallon of freezing water upon a Water Cure patient as they stood below – this autumn it will again – with brave participants sponsored for charity.

Water Cure demonstrations, hell fire preachers, Victorian photography, street theatre, a Victorian Fair, bell ringers, well dressing, Victorian suppers, old time music hall, hog roasts, even the Ebbw Vale Male Voice Choir are some other attractions.

September 6 199X

For further information contact Ian Phillipson (01886) 885032 (Ideas that Sell Publicity)

Fig. 3. Another illustrated release with text flowing round the image.

Ideally it would be satisfying to see your release used verbatim, or nearly so. The chances are that it won't be. Most likely it will be used in part, or more probably, just form the structure of a story that's written entirely by someone else. However, it doesn't really matter as long as the story is used and is correct.

LAYING OUT YOUR PRESS RELEASE

In part, through common sense or long-term practice, a number of rules and a standard layout have evolved for the press release. Though the importance of these is frequently overstated (it would take a really fussy and incompetent journalist to ignore a good story simply because a press release was not laid out in the traditional manner), it's sensible to follow common practice. These are the 'rules':

Some basic guidelines

- Every press release should be printed or typed, unless you are going for a creative and unusual effect.

- Every press release should have a headline at the top of the page. This should be written in capital letters. It should not be underlined.

- The first line of the first paragraph should be justified to the left, that is flush with the left margin.

- The first line of all subsequent paragraphs should be indented to the right. A five character indent is adequate.

- An empty line should be inserted between paragraphs.

- All text should be justified to the left and not fully justified. This will make the text ragged on the right and flush on the left.

- All the text should be double spaced to allow for corrections and editing marks to be made between lines and in the margins. This is probably less important than previously now that so much editing is done on computer. However, it does make the release clearer to read.

- So that the release doesn't look cramped on the page, margins should be at least an inch on either side, with an inch and a half at the bottom.

- A press release should be short, but long enough to do its job. Keep it to one side of A4 (if possible) and ideally no more than three sides. Plain white A4 is fine for the second and third sheets, though you can

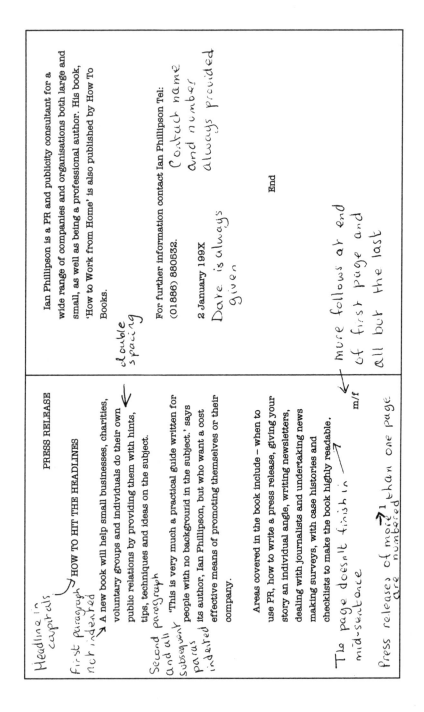

Fig. 4. The layout of a press release.

use specially designed 'run on' paper which may have a logo but no address or phone details. If you can't quite fit the release on one sheet of paper, try one and a half line spacing and not double.

- If the release runs to more than one page type m/f (more follows) at the bottom of the page, except on the last page of the release, and number each page.

- If the release runs to more than one page include a catchline (an explanatory phrase that relates to the release title) at the top of subsequent pages. For instance, if the title of your release is NEW CATNIP MOUSE DEVELOPED then the catchline could be 'Mouse' or 'Catnip Mouse'.

- If the release runs to more than one page, received wisdom says that you should not carry a sentence over from one page to the next.

- After the final paragraph of the story give a contact name and telephone number where journalists can go for further information.

- At the bottom of the final page write 'end' or 'END'.

- Below 'end' give the date on which the release was issued.

Using computer software
If you feel your writing skills aren't good enough to create workable press releases, then you might find helpful the software, 'Do-it-yourself PR Business', produced by CCA Software. This holds 100 press release templates which cover most situations a small business might require. All you do is fill in the blank spaces in the release then print it out. There are even instructions on how best to complete each release and where to send it for best effect.

Being 'different'
Having told you the 'proper' way to write a press release, sometimes it is good to be different and really stand out on the journalist's desk. Press releases have been written on, or accompanied by, Wellington boots, bricks, boomerangs and much stranger items.

If you choose this route then make sure the angle is relevant to the story, and don't be too cryptic or wayout just for the sake of it. A journalist will want to know what the story is about quickly, so don't mislead or string them along.

Checking your work
Whenever you send out written material representing your organisation, it should be as free as humanly possible from spelling

mistakes and grammatical errors. This is particularly important in a short document such as a press release where errors can really stand out. In particular, run a **spellcheck** (if you use a word processor) for words that become rude or embarrassing when a letter has been missed out. Public becoming pubic would be one example, but there are others that are far worse.

YOUR PRESS RELEASE CHECKLIST

	Yes	*No*
1. Does the release have a headline?	____	____
2. Does the release 'give the game away' in the first paragraph?	____	____
3. Is the release double spaced?	____	____
4. Does the release cover less than two sides of A4?	____	____
5. Have you put in too much technical material that would be better in a backgrounder?	____	____
6. Have you given a contact name and number?	____	____
7. Have you checked for spelling and grammatical mistakes?	____	____

ISSUING PRESS RELEASES

Don't assume your release will be passed orf to the right journalist – the chances are that it won't be.

You need to send it to the right person in the first place. On local newspapers this will be the editor; on national newspapers the news editor; on small publications the editor; on larger publications this will be either the editor, news editor or specialist correspondent; and on trade publications the editor, news editor or specialist correspondent.

Some publications have regular features or columns on specific themes which are put together by a specific journalist, who may be interested in your story; others may have special interest sections which either appear daily or perhaps once a week. *The Sunday Times* for example has a small business section and Innovations column, while *The Guardian* publishes its Media Pages on Mondays.

If it's appropriate always try to include a photograph to back up your release. Editors are always looking for visual images to reinforce their stories. If you don't have the budget for it, then don't send a photo with every release. Instead, insert a line on the press release which reads 'Telephone (contact name and phone number) for prints and negatives of (the subject)'. There's more on photography for PR in Chapter 6.

Action tip

Periodically contact national newspapers to find out if they are preparing a supplement or features on your particular area of interest. If they are, there may be the opportunity for you to appear.

WORKING TO LEAD TIMES

Whenever you send out any material to the press, either a release, or article, it is vitally important to be aware and knowledgeable about lead times. It always takes time to edit your submitted copy and produce the publication. Newspapers may only require words and pictures the day before, or even on the day of publication, but some magazines may need the copy several months before they hit the newsstands. This is known as **lead time** and you must be aware of it.

It is no good supplying information about an event two weeks before to a publication that has already been completely written for the last month and it is just about to come back from the printers.

To find out the lead time of a publication, simply phone up the editorial office and ask. You don't need to talk to anyone senior, an editorial assistant or even the receptionist (on small publications) should be able to help you.

Keeping records

Keep copies of all the releases you send out and a list of the publications and journalists to which they've been sent, and the dates.

Either write the names directly onto a copy of the release, or print out a list and staple this to the release. Alternatively you can develop a more formal submission listing such as the one shown in Figure 5.

Example: Alan learns a hard lesson

Alan runs an electronic components company which wins a contract that's important to the firm, but hardly large enough or interesting enough to interest anyone else. Undaunted by that fact, Alan cobbles together what he thinks is a press release and then sends out copies to any publication he can think of.

After a week of waiting by the phone for calls from fascinated journalists, Alan's patience runs out. He starts ringing round the magazines and papers to find out what's happening to his story. The result is nothing. Those journalists he does get in touch with have

Press Release subject – Victorian weekend

Angle	Sent to	Date
General interest	Midlands Today (tv)	0.6.06.9x
	Central Today (tv)	"
	BBC Hereford & Worcester	"
	Radio Wyvern	"
	Severnsound (radio)	"
Rural enjoyment	Country Life	"
	Country Living	"
	This England	"
Medical aspects	Your Health & Lifestyle	09.09.9X
	Health Now	"
	Here's Health	"
Holiday possibilities	BBC Holidays	"
	Getting about Britain	"
	Holiday UK	"
	Travel UK	"
	Active Life	"
	Choice	"
	Fifty Plus	"
Women's involvement	Woman's Hour	"
	My Weekly	"
	Woman	"
Children's involvement	Blue Peter	"
	Early Times	"

Fig. 5. Keeping a record of mailed out press releases.

already binned Alan's release and no amount of wheedling or persuasion on his part will induce them to run the story.

In the end, Alan starts berating the journalists for not investigating further. This attitude is counter productive because the only journalist who was thinking about following it up is so irritated by Alan, that what would in any case have been a minor story, is binned.

So, unless you know a journalist, don't follow up press releases, a release should stand – or fall – on it own merits. If it's good enough it will run without the call.

FOLLOWING YOUR STORY IN THE PRESS

Don't expect, and never ask, a publication to provide you with a cutting of your story should they run it. They might tell you they will, but ninety-nine times out of a hundred they won't. Why should they? They have better things to do. If you want cuttings you'll either have to keep a careful watch on the relevant publications or employ a cuttings service to monitor the press for you.

HOW TO EMBARGO A PRESS RELEASE

An **embargo** is a time and date before which a press release cannot be published. On the whole journalists don't like embargoes because they go against their natural inclination to publish what they know. And there's no guarantee that an embargo will be obeyed. You will not in any case be able to apply an embargo to a hard news story. If news has already been made then you cannot expect the press to sit on it.

To embargo a press release simply type 'NOT FOR PUBLICA-TION UNTIL (DATE)' or 'EMBARGOED UNTIL (DATE)' at the top of the press release. Don't make this embargo too long or the press will either ignore it, or simply lose interest in the story. And never embargo stories that don't need it. That just makes you and your story laughable.

When to embargo

For the most part you will never need to use an embargo, but there will be occasions. Embargoes are most commonly used:

- if the story you're sending out is long or complex and involves the journalist in further background research to develop it;

- if the release contains the text of a speech which you don't want revealed before it's made. An embargo helps ensure the text goes out at the same time or shortly after the speech is made;

- if you're inviting a celebrity to an event and want the press there, but don't want that information publicly revealed until then to retain the surprise element. You won't be able to put an embargo on the event itself;

- if you don't wish the event to be covered by certain sections of the media. For instance, if you don't want the story covered in the Sunday papers, you would embargo it until the Monday, which is generally a quiet news day.

BACKGROUNDERS – THE RELEASE'S FRIEND

Press releases aren't the place to cram in every fact and figure about your company, organisation or event. If you feel journalists would benefit from knowing more about the history and circumstances behind your story, then supply a backgrounder. These should provide journalists with the information they need to answer follow up questions without having to research elsewhere, or make time consuming phone calls to you. Having that information immediately to hand could make all the difference between the story being run or not.

What to include

Information contained in a backgrounder can include history about the company (when it was established), location, personnel, employee numbers, financial background, other product areas, charitable work and sponsorships.

Backgrounders can be written on plain sheets of white A4 paper. Head them with a suitable title that outlines their content, such as 'Biographical Details', then present the information pretty much as it would appear on a press release (double spaced and a line between paragraphs). There are no special rules as to how a backgrounder should be written and laid out. Staple the sheets of each backgrounder together in the top left corner. If you are supplying several backgrounders at one time then don't attach them together.

MAKING PHONE CONTACTS

If you have a story that needs selling quickly, or one that you want in before the publication's deadline, you can contact editorial offices by phone. If you know the name of a journalist who you feel would be particularly interested in your story then ask for the person by name.

If not then approach those to whom you would normally have sent a press release (see **Issuing press releases** above). Ask for their name from the switchboard or reception.

When you get through, explain the story, simply and concisely, emphasising why you think it's newsworthy. Again, don't be self indulgent. If the journalist expresses no interest, thank them and try another publication. Never lose your temper at their 'stupidity in not being able to recognise a good story when they hear one...' (Likewise, never be tempted to phone up a journalist and rage at them for not using your story. This is *not* the way to build up a long-term relationship with the press.)

Leaving messages

If you can't get through to the journalist you want and are asked to leave your name, don't expect editors or journalists to return your call, some will and some won't. Say you'll phone back. This leaves you in control. Such gentle persistence will see you getting through, though never persist until the point of being a nuisance.

5
How to Write a PR Article

'The pen is mightier than the sword'. Edward George Bulwer Lytton.

WHY PR ARTICLES ARE IMPORTANT

While press releases throw the emphasis of writing onto journalists, writing articles yourself for publication allows you to maintain greater control of the message you want to put across.

The advantage to an editor of using a PR article is that it's free and that brightens their hearts considerably. However, if an article is well written, relevant to the readership, interesting and suitable for the market, then there is no reason why you couldn't submit it as a freelance writer. In which case if it is published you are paid.

The disadvantages of writing PR articles are that they take time and that you have to have good writing skills.

WHAT MAKES A GOOD PR ARTICLE?

PR articles are no different from any other sort of article so they must meet the same criteria. That is, they must be:

- well written. An editor, even of a low quality publication in desperate need of copy, will not run poorly written material. And whereas a press release may be re-written by an in-house journalist, an editor will not expect to re-write a submitted article, except for some gentle tidying up. If a wholesale re-write is required, then unless the content of the piece is really worthwhile, it will be consigned to the bin. No one in an editorial office has the time, or inclination to rescue a bad piece.

- relevant. Again, just like with a press release, an article must be of interest to the readership.

- interesting. Articles that have nothing to say will not be printed. Lively quotes, surprising facts and figures, intriguing anecdotes and the right angle will all play their part in achieving an enthusiastic editorial reception.

● on time. If you ever make a promise to an editor to supply their publication with copy or information, then keep it. Editors and journalists must meet deadlines and if you don't behave in the same way then they will lose confidence in you, your company and your abilities. Also you must keep to the brief you are given. Going off at a tangent and doing your own thing will surprise the editor and probably result in the piece not being used.

The style of the article

There are two basic approaches to writing a PR article. First, you can present it as a personal piece in which you put forward your expert and informed view on the subject. This role enhances your reputation and gives you additional credibility. You may well receive a name check at the bottom of the piece, with some information on your business and its relevance to the readership and your ability to write on the subject.

Second, you can write the feature as a balanced piece in which you take an impartial view, bringing in other organisations and companies for comparison and to back up your arguments. If you do this, the companies you choose should be in some way different from your own organisation so you aren't giving direct competitors a plug. For sure you will have to downgrade your own importance, but the result's a more balanced piece.

HOW TO APPROACH AN EDITOR

Targeting the right publication

If you think that you have a good article idea that will help your PR, first, list potential publications that are likely to be interested in the piece. Find out a little about each by consulting a directory such as *The Writer's Handbook*, or the *Writers' and Artists' Yearbook*. These will generally indicate the best way to approach the editor, most of whom will want to see a query letter which outlines the nature of the article. In this you'll indicate what the piece will be about, why it's of interest to readers now, how long the article will be, and why you are well qualified to write it.

Introducing yourself

At this point you can indicate your direct interest in the piece, saying that you don't want paying for the article. This may or may not appeal to the editor who may be suspicious of your motives and ability to produce a balanced article. You can provide some reassurance by enclosing tear sheets of your articles that have already been published.

The query letter should be sent out in a DL business envelope, though you may like to use a larger envelope if you are enclosing a number of tear sheets or photocopies. When you send out your query letter also include a SAE for a reply.

Following the editor's brief

If successful, the editor will either phone or write to give you the go ahead on the piece, indicating how long the article should be, what exactly it should be about and the deadline for its submission. You ignore these instructions at your peril.

Making multiple submissions

You now have an agreement with the publication to supply them with copy. So, tempting though it might be to think of it running in several magazines at once you can't submit your article elsewhere. The only time you can submit simultaneously is if you're submitting to non-competing publications with different readerships. This is unlikely to be the case with national publications, but it is possible if you are targeting publications that cover only local areas with a specific group of local readers.

Of course there is nothing to stop you sending out similar but different articles for publication to competing journals. Once you have developed a 'stock' article, you can develop and alter it, coming up with fresh angles and styles of writing. A good writer should be able to transform the same facts into totally different pieces to suit different publications.

Example

Take a look at Figure 6. It's a query letter written by a computer distributor looking to generate increased usage in laptop computers by suggesting possible ways in which they could be used. This query was sent out first to writers' magazines and then on to a few general interest publications and not too technical computer titles.

Notice how the letter doesn't mention that Jason was after publicity for his business. If the piece is accepted he will of course give his business as a contact, as well as some other companies that he doesn't see as a threat. Indeed, to increase the credibility of his company, Jason even set up a Writers Advisory Service to help authors choose their ideal machine.

```
John Constable
Editor
The Daily Writer
London

7 September 199X

Dear John Constable

    Do writers need to be tied to their studies, offices and kitchen tables
to produce good words?

    I don't think so.

    This letter, as well as numerous articles, several video scripts and a
book were written sitting on a sun-drenched bench half way up a hill
overlooking the beautiful Herefordshire countryside all thanks to a laptop
computer (all of this was true by the way). As far as I am concerned I
have produced more and better work by getting away from the office, at
least for some of the time.

    Would you be interested in a piece that explored this idea? It could
look at how you can derive inspiration by leaving the office behind,
whether you are writing fact or fiction; how to choose a laptop that is
right for you; where to go to write: if you're writing a feature on railways
then why not go to a railway station, and create the piece in the very
environment you're writing about?

    I think the piece would make about 1,000 words, though you may
have other ideas. I would of course submit on spec.

    I have edited several computer magazines so have a good technical
understanding of the subject as well as the writing skills. Sae enclosed.

Yours sincerely


Jason Harrison
```

Fig. 6. An example query letter.

Action tip

Think of five subjects relating to your business or organisation that
would be suitable for development into PR articles.

1. ....

2. ....

3. ....

4. ....

5. ....

HOW TO WRITE THE ARTICLE

Public relations is a communications business, and the better you are at writing, the greater will be your success. Unlike press releases which are really a form of 'manufactured' writing, articles require better than average writing skills if they are to be of a publishable standard. These skills can be learned and you should make a concerted attempt to improve the quality and speed of your writing.

As mentioned so many times before, in PR how people perceive you is crucially important, and poorly written and uninteresting material reflects badly on you if you submit it to an editor. This is particularly so if you're supplying a number of sponsored articles because you'll need to keep up the quality of the words throughout the series and to be able to generate a variety of interesting ideas.

But since this is not a book on how to write articles, it's assumed you either already have these skills or are willing to put in the hours to acquire them. As with most things practise does make perfect so there is nothing better than writing to make you improve. There are any number of good books on article writing that will help you on the way. In the meantime, if you feel you do have the skills, but perhaps lack the impetus and fluency to produce words quickly and effectively the following techniques and methods may help.

Basic techniques for article writing

- Don't create a formal outline for an article. If you find it difficult to get going, don't try and start at the beginning, but anywhere you feel comfortable. You can put points in the right order later, using cut and paste facilities if you work on a computer.

- Once you have started writing just keep going. Get as many words down on paper or on screen as you can. Worry about revising them later. Don't try to get each sentence right before moving on to the next. When working on a computer or WP, don't spellcheck as you go along, but leave this until the very end, otherwise the writing flow is broken.

- Write something down even if you lack the facts. Just make a note on screen or paper to find out about that later, you don't want to be researching in the middle of a writing session.

- Create imaginary deadlines for yourself and work against them. Tell yourself that you will have written 500 words by three o'clock. Work against a clockwork timer, aiming to write so many words in forty minutes or so.

- If you leave written work over to the next day, know what you are going to write about first thing in the morning.

- When you have finished your first draft put it away for a few days then come back to it.

HOW TO SUBMIT YOUR ARTICLE

Type up or print your work double spaced on white 80gm paper. Leave plenty of margins on all sides and number each page. A catchline should be on every page after the title page. Send all the pages flat in a C4 envelope. If you are submitting on spec, that is without a commission from the editor, then include a self addressed stamped envelope for the article if it's not required.

As well as providing hard copy on paper, many publications are increasingly willing to take copy submitted electronically on computer disk or down the telephone line via modem. It is worth offering this ability to editors if it increases your chances of publication.

Offering a list of PR articles

Why stop at supplying just a single feature to a publication? Why not a whole series? Generally this will be a series of articles on different subjects but with a single theme with you receiving a name check and background about you at the end of each one. If you think a series is the way forward for you then:

- draw up a list of suitable publications to approach;

- prepare a list of potential article ideas, with a few lines of explanation about each;

- write a letter to each editor suggesting the idea of a series of free articles and outline your suitability for writing these features;

- include a photocopy or tear sheets of your published work. These are your credentials and show your writing skills;

- include a short backgrounder on yourself which highlights your skills, specialities and career history, all reinforcing your suitability to write articles.

There can be some resistance to these 'sponsored' articles from a publication's advertising manager who views this high level of PR activity with suspicion because it would be reducing the sales department's revenue. However, for an editor, sponsored articles are money savers – quality editorial for free.

HOW TO USE READERS' LETTERS

They may be the poor man's article and therefore fairly low on your list of promotional possibilities, but readers' letters should not be forgotten as they do have their own particular PR role. Not only will your name (and perhaps your organisation) appear, but others can also mention your name in follow up letters in later weeks.

Readers' letters can be particularly useful to correct inaccuracies that have appeared in the press. If used for this then they should not repeat the original inaccuracy, thus letting people who haven't read the original correspondence know what it is about.

They don't take long to write and if interesting have a good chance of being published, And, if you aim at the right publication they can generate a lot of enquiries for you.

Readers' letters can be either reactive (you respond to news stories covered in previous issues) or proactive (you start a new subject that you believe will be of interest to readers). In either case they should be short and make their point quickly. Those that are too long will only be cut by a sub-editor who, worse still, may not even bother to read your 'essay' in the first place.

All letters should be relevant to the readership of the publication. They must be grammatically correct (even if it's presumed you aren't a professional writer, bad spelling and English reflect badly on you) and contain no jargon, or an angry diatribe (though a certain degree of emotion can be used, depending on the subject). They should also not be on controversial issues such as religion or race.

Action tip
Begin looking through the readers' letters pages of the local, specialist or national press. Is there an issue you feel strongly about that you could develop with a reader's letter? What would be the main argument of your letter? Write it here:

....

....

....

....

```
The Daily Trumpeter
Trumpeter Towers
London

17 October 199X

Dear Sir

There are several inaccuracies in your report (23 June, 199X)
regarding our Victoria Road property development. What I said to
your reporter was that the development would not be detrimental
to local property prices. Secondly, that there had been only one
objection to the planning application, which has been widely
welcomed by those living in the area. These two facts alter the
whole argument of your case.

Yours faithfully


Karen Bloggins
Managing Director
Bloggins Developments
```

Fig. 7. A straightforward reader's letter.

Example: Anne gets her mother to write

Readers' letters don't need always to come from you. To launch her
travellers' introduction service (which puts people who want to go on
holiday but don't have anyone to go with in touch with similar
people) Anne asked her mother to write to the letters page of a
woman's magazine. In this she extolled the virtues of the service and
what it was all about.

A few weeks later Anne received a call from the researcher on the
magazine who wanted to know more. A month or two after that
Anne's mother's letter was published and resulted in over 700
enquiries! And all for the cost of a second class stamp: slightly
devious perhaps, but highly cost effective PR.

POINTS FOR DISCUSSION

1. Do you feel you have the right skills for successful article writing?
   If not, how could you get some help?

2. Draft a letter you could send to several editors, offering them a
   series of free articles on a certain subject.

3. Draft out a short 'backgrounder' about yourself.

6
Using Photography in PR

'Every picture paints a story.' Advertisement for Sloan's Backache and Kidney Oils, 1907.

DOES YOUR STORY NEED A PHOTOGRAPH?

Yes, whenever possible, because pictures sell stories to editors. Even a really bland photograph can be better than nothing, but wherever possible a photo should enhance the story, not simply be thrown in for good measure.

There will be times when it is particularly important to accompany your press release with a photograph, such as when explaining a new product or item. It is far easier to show someone what it is you make rather than describing it to them. The more technical or innovative the product the more likely you are to benefit from including a picture.

Mono or colour?
Though colour is increasingly being used by newspapers, most still print in black and white and so require mono shots.

On the other hand, magazines and the trade press can be great users of colour photographs. Colour transparencies are often requested because they give the best reproduction, though many publishers are now able to achieve good colour reproduction from prints. Colour negatives can be converted to black and white if you need to produce cheaply a larger number of photographs. Black and white shots will not be converted to colour.

When you provide PR shots do not expect to have your transparencies or prints returned even if you request them. It is wise therefore to have duplicates (dupes) made of the original transparency, though there will be some quality loss in these and they are expensive. As a cost effective alternative ask the photographer to take a number of similar shots of the same subject.

PROFESSIONAL PHOTOGRAPHY OR DIY?

Whenever possible, public relations and publicity shots should be taken by a professional photographer, since sending shots of the holiday snap variety just won't impress a hard bitten editor one little bit. Once more, image is all important and if you send out shoddy images of your products and personnel, then what are the general public, or your potential customers going to think about you? Probably that you're shoddy too, and what's more, you can't be bothered (or worse still don't care) to get this right.

It may be tempting to think you can do the job, but it's best left to a professional, unless you are far more than just a competent snapper.

How to find a photographer

Photographers will advertise their services in the *Yellow Pages*, trade magazines and 'professional' sources of information such as *The Creative Handbook* and *Hollis Press and Public Relations Annual*. Local newspapers will also carry the names of staff photographers who may be willing to do a little moonlighting for you.

Karen learns from experience

Karen has a small budget and needs some PR shots, but knows she can't take them herself. A friend suggests that she contact a photographer on the local newspaper, which she does. The photographer says he's done jobs like this before, no problem.

Problem: the news photographer, though competent, is used to obtaining shots quickly and with limited set up. He doesn't take as much time as he ought over setting up and getting the lighting just right. The photographs turn out rather dull and certainly unimaginative.

This taught Karen several lessons. First, that you only get what you pay for and second always check a photographer's portfolio to see if they really can produce the kind of shots you are after.

Checking the cost

Your photographic requirements will have three elements to them: the time the photographer takes to do the job (an average rate is £60-80 per hour and £200-230 per day); the cost of materials (rolls of film cost only a couple of pounds); and the printing up of photographs (bulk printing is around £1.50 for each colour shot and 60-70p for black and white).

HOW TO TAKE BETTER PR PHOTOGRAPHS

Basic guidelines

If budgets are tight you might have no other choice but to take publicity photographs yourself. These guidelines should help you obtain better results:

- Use equipment that can do the job. Most modern cameras, even the simplest 'click and go' ones will do an adequate job. Good lighting can make or break a picture, but this is an area in which many amateurs fall down. You'll need appropriate flash lamps and fill-in lights if the subject is to be properly lit.

- Take more shots than you need, making minor adjustments in terms of position and by bracketing the shot. That is using different apertures and speeds, perhaps taking some shots at F5.6 and others at F8.

- Don't be afraid of posing people for the best effect. When you are the photographer you are in charge, so you can be pleasantly bossy.

- Get in close to the subject so that the subject fills the viewfinder and the picture frame.

- If you are photographing people or products indoors, then you can create a good effect by shooting them in front of a pale coloured background. Rolls of white paper can be hung up behind the subject and on the floor to achieve the right effect.

- Take both landscape (horizontal) and portrait (vertical) format shots of the subject then you can offer a choice of shots to editors, if the budget allows.

- Remove distracting objects out of shot, so they don't pull the eye towards them.

People shots – how to take them

Head and shoulder shots of people are the ones generally required for PR purposes since you'll need them when supplying stories on new staff appointments, significant achievements, retirements and promotions.

Avoid taking these photographs with the person square on to the camera; pose them so that they stand with their shoulders turned slightly away from the camera with their head looking full into the lens. Don't take shots full on, and be careful about spectacles – the lenses can reflect a flash or other light source.

Group photographs are more complicated since they can be

excruciatingly boring at the best of times. They need a little imagination in the way that people are posed and the locations in which they're put. Try to incorporate a prop or something that links them or you with the business, your event or organisation.

Checklists – shots to avoid

If you can answer yes then your PR photograph might be in danger of being hackneyed or clichéd.

	Yes	No
1. Does the shot feature a large group of people, posed or not?	___	___
2. Are people pretending to do something they are obviously not good at or unaccustomed to?	___	___
3. Are staff just sitting in front of a computer?	___	___
4. Are people smiling at each other as they meet in totally false circumstances?	___	___
5. Are they sitting at their desk with pens poised?	___	___
6. Are directors handing over giant cheques to charities?	___	___
7. Are there scantily clad female models who have no relevance to the story or product?	___	___

Increasing the drama of a photograph

The more predictable and run of the mill your photographs, the less impact they will have and the more likely they are to be rejected by a harassed editor. Use your imagination and be creative when coming up with shots.

- If your product is small, try heaping them together. Great numbers of anything create dramatic images. If you're a widget manufacturer pile one million of them into a mountain.

- Create contrasts. Combine the soft with the hard, wet with the dry, small with the large – an elephant with a mouse, feathers with hard metal, water with sand.

- Create unusual collections of objects. This type of image gives the eye a lot to feast upon as it explores and lingers on the grouping.

- Photograph things from unusual angles, but be careful of making the photograph so unusual that the reader's eye can't be bothered to unravel the visual mystery.

- Make something big look small, or something small look big. If you photograph a subject by looking up at it, then it will appear larger than it actually is. The reverse is true if you climb up a step ladder and take a photograph looking down.

- Put something in an unusual setting. Again, if properly done this can be eye catching and intriguing.

- Enhance an object's size, or lack of it, by using another well known object to highlight its dimensions. For instance, a human hand holding a microchip is an image that emphasises the small size of the circuitry.

- Photographs can be particularly effective in grabbing the attention if they feature a famous person, are funny, or dramatic, or contain something that is unexpected.

How to improve your camera skills

Take photographs regularly. If you only pick up a camera every now and then you can't expect to be good. Practise. Read books and magazines about photography and keep an eye open for unusual shots and ideas that you might be able to copy. Join a local camera club.

If you take your own publicity shots, be self critical and honest about their quality. If they just aren't up to scratch you will have to employ a professional or let someone else within the firm or organisation take them.

HOW TO CAPTION PHOTOGRAPHS AND ILLUSTRATIONS

The right place

Every photograph or illustration should have a caption attached to it. Never write this on the back of the photographs. No matter how lightly you do it there's always the danger that the pen or pencil will make an impression that comes through on the face of the picture.

Instead, write, or preferably type or print the caption onto a strip of paper or label, and stick this to the back of the photograph. Use Spray Mount or Cow Gum to do this. The caption can also be attached with sticky tape by its top edge to the photo's back.

The right information

Information on the caption should be sufficient to explain what's

```
┌─────────────────────────────────────────────────────────┐
│                                                         │
│         ANYTOWN'S UNICYCLE HOCKEY TOURNAMENT            │
│                                                         │
│  LOCATION: Anytown, Anytownshire                        │
│  DATE: 17 September 199X                                │
│                                                         │
│  Unicycle hockey is a fast moving sport full of thrills,│
│  spills, single wheels and narrow saddles. It's         │
│  Britain's fastest growing one-wheeled sport and is     │
│  already played by members of the Royal Family. The     │
│  Anytown Tournament will be the first of its kind in    │
│  the country.                                           │
│                                                         │
│      This event will offer a great photo-opportunity    │
│  for ABC Sports Magazine. If you would like to attend,  │
│  or send a photographer, then arrange your press pass   │
│  by calling Alan Onewheel Tel 012 345 6789.             │
│                                                         │
└─────────────────────────────────────────────────────────┘
```

Fig. 8. An invitation to a photo-opportunity.

happening in the photograph and who or what is involved. A contact name and telephone number should be given and a catchline supplied. The caption should contain a mini-summary of the press release so that if pictures and words become separated the story can still be run.

Normally photographs will accompany a press release and so be sent to the news or feature editor. However, if the photograph is particularly striking then it may be worth sending a copy photograph to the picture editor, especially if there is no real substance to the accompanying story.

HOW TO INVITE PRESS PHOTOGRAPHERS

There will be times when you don't want to organise the PR photography for yourself but rather invite press photographers along. If you've sent out a press release then the editor may already have arranged for a photographer to accompany a journalist to your event or launch. At other times there won't be much of a story but a good picture opportunity which a photographer could deal with alone. If that's the case then send out a photo-opportunity invitation such as the one below. This is similar to a standard press release, though with an emphasis on the visual imagery. The first paragraph outlines the event, while the second adds detail.

A PR PHOTOGRAPHY CHECKLIST

	Yes	No

1. Have you chosen a suitable location for photography before the photographer arrives? ____ ____

2. Is the location clear of rubbish and tidy? (If a lot of lifting is needed to do this, make sure someone strong is on hand. People who are to appear in the shot dressed in their best clothes should be spared this muscular effort, unless you want them to look hot, sweaty and dishevelled in the photograph.) ____ ____

3. Is everyone who is to appear in the photograph available when the photographer is due to arrive? ____ ____

4. Is everyone to hand when the photographer does arrive? ____ ____

5. Is everyone suitably dressed to convey the right image? ____ ____

6. Is the location clear of everyone who doesn't need to be there? (The last thing you want is an audience that can make the subject of the photograph nervous, the tension will show. There is also always a tendency for onlookers to try to put people off.) ____ ____

7. Do you have all the props you need for the photograph? ____ ____

POINTS FOR DISCUSSION

1. Choose a subject for a PR photograph. What props would you use to add interest to the picture?

2. Could you acquire the basic photographic equipment and practical skills to take PR photographs?

3. Think of three PR stories your organisation could develop, and plan a set of photographs to accompany them.

7
How to Talk to Journalists

'You cannot hope to bribe or twist
Thank God! the British Journalist.
But seeing what they will do unbribed,
there's no occasion to.'
   Humbert Wolfe, *The Celestial City*

SHOULD YOU AGREE TO BE INTERVIEWED?

What a question after spending so much time trying to capture the interest of the media, sending out press releases and writing PR articles! But there may well be times when discretion is the better part of valour.

So, with every approach for an interview the first basic question to yourself must be, do I want to be interviewed? And no matter how much effort you have put in to generating press interest, there may be times when you don't want to talk with journalists.

Reasons for refusing an interview
You may decide not to talk to journalists:

- if you fear being misrepresented

- if you don't have the time

- if you think the programme or publication is unsuitable for your PR needs

- if you don't want publicity at all

- or if you don't want any publicity right now.

HOW TO BE INTERVIEWED

Some general rules
Journalists want information from you. How they go about obtaining it and how you present it to them depend on whether they are from

magazines and newspapers or radio and television. Each will make their own demands upon you, though the techniques for dealing with them are broadly the same.

Do your homework
First, find out as much as you can about the interview beforehand. How long will it take? What areas will be covered? Who will do the interviewing? For radio and television programmes will the interview be live or recorded? What is the style of the publication or programme? (If you don't know, then ask what type of people read or watch it.) Find out why the journalist is calling. Is it in response to a press release or something else, such as a mention in the press? If so, ask them to fax you the cutting.

Preparing properly
Second, prepare for every interview as though it's the most important in the world. Think of possible questions and work out your answers to them. Being interviewed, particularly if live on television, is not without its potential risks so you need to be really thoroughly prepared.

Decide your priorities
Third, before the interview, go over your notes and decide on the main points you want to make; choose any statistics you want to use. Review the press releases you have sent out.

Have some anecdotes ready
Fourth, think of relevant anecdotes that illustrate your main points. People like these stories, listen to them and remember them. If an idea is complicated or unusual, try to think of an analogy that will make it more concrete and understandable.

Show interest
Fifth, when the interview begins concentrate on what is being asked. Show you are interested in the journalist's questions.

Be discreet
Sixth, be discreet. Don't disengage brain from mouth when talking to anyone in a television crew, even if it looks as though they may have come along for the ride. This is especially true if you are being interviewed about a problem or a controversy. It is not unknown for interviewers to overhear and throw the secret information at you while on air.

To be quoted or not?

Sometimes you'll want to provide background information for the press, to help their understanding but without you being identified as the source. This propels us squarely into the realms of 'off the record comments' and 'non-attributable quotes'.

Going off the record

Going off the record means you say something to a journalist, which you don't want to be published. You must tell the journalist that what you are about to say is off the record and get their agreement to this before saying anything. Off the record comments are usually honoured, but there's no guarantee that an unscrupulous or desperate journalist won't use your remarks.

Giving a non-attributable quote

With a non-attributable quote you make it clear that you want information published, but without the source of it revealed. Should you offer a non-attributable quote, agree with the journalist how this fact will be indicated. Will you be a source within the company, an insider, or a member of the committee? Make sure that this attribution is sufficiently vague so you can't be identified, a quote that's attributed to 'a spokesman for the two man company' tends to give the game away!

A checklist of traps for interviewees

	Yes	*No*
1. Is the journalist apparently not paying attention to what you are saying? (They could be trying to get you to say something more exciting.)	____	____
2. Has the journalist closed his or her notebook? (They can still listen to your gaffes. Watch your tongue whenever talking to the press.)	____	____
3. Is the journalist being very sympathetic? (They may just be wanting you to grasp their proffered hand of friendship and pour out your heart to them so they can write a better story.)	____	____
4. Are they using manufactured quotes, such as 'Wouldn't you agree that...?'		

	Yes	*No*
(Never say simply 'yes' or 'no' to this, even if you agree. Respond with something like 'I wouldn't put it quite that way' and then go on to answer the question in your own words.)	___	___

5. Is the journalist trying to read upside down the documents that are in front of you?

6. Is the journalist asking the same question again and again, only in a slightly different way each time? (By nagging away in this manner the journalist is looking for a chink in your armour. Answering the question in the way that you answered its very similar brother.)

7. Is the journalist repeating an allegation made by someone else? (If you deny the allegation then you set yourself up for a story that begins 'Allegations of corruption were yesterday denied by the Managing Director of Bloggins Flowers.' There was never a story in the first place, but lo and behold one has been created. To handle this situation go off the record immediately and tell the journalist the circumstances behind the story, and why there is nothing there worth writing about.)

HOW TO DEAL WITH RADIO INTERVIEWS

The growth in numbers of local radio stations has created great opportunities. There are three ways in which you can give a radio interview: at the radio studio; at an outside location; and down the phone.

Attending a studio interview

Studio based radio interviews are less formal than their TV counterparts. You'll find the studio is air conditioned with a soundproofed glass. You'll sit at a table or desk with a microphone, rather like an angle poise lamp, nearby to catch your every word. If you are asked to wear headphones keep them on one ear only so you'll be able to hear better the tone and pitch of your own voice.

After an off air sound test of your voice (say anything, it doesn't matter), the presenter will introduce you and the interview will begin.

Concentrate on the interviewer and ignore everything else around. This can be difficult as you may see researchers or the producers moving behind the glass window. Keep as still as you can in the studio – flailing arms can easily hit microphones. One last thing, especially on local radio expect music to be played between questions.

Unlike the other 'physical' medium of television you don't need to worry about cameras or too much about the way you look, though if you turn up looking scruffy rather than smartly dressed this could influence the way in which the interviewer goes about his or her job. However, studio microphones in particular are very sensitive, so avoid 'noisy' clothing, such as creaky, crackling leather jackets which will make listeners think more about bondage than the seriousness of your message.

Attending a location interview

These are pretty straightforward and can be done at your office, factory or out in the countryside or street. Remember radio journalists will be trying to paint a sound picture so the more relevant sounds you can offer them the better.

Giving a phone interview

Many interviews for radio are now done over the phone because it's cheap to do and convenient. They are usually arranged at short notice with a journalist just phoning up in response to a press release for instance, and asking for an interview. If this happens to you, the first rule is don't panic, quickly followed by the second rule which is, do not agree to be interviewed immediately. Even if you are well prepared, ask them to call back in 20–30 minutes and take that time to put your mind in gear.

Preventing disturbances

Make sure you won't be disturbed during the interview. If you work in an office, warn other staff when the interview will be taking place. The last thing you want is a secretary blundering into the room with a cheery 'here's your tea and digestives', mid-way through the interview, especially if it's going out live. To make doubly sure, write 'Radio interview in progress. Quiet Please', on a sheet of paper and stick it to the outside of your office door.

Avoiding background noise

In some commercial or industrial environments, there's bound to be background noise, but you needn't worry too much about this, especially if it helps set the scene. If you work from home, tell the family to be quiet, close the door and windows to the room to mask outside sounds. Shut pets away. If you have barking dogs farm them out to neighbours for a while. As an added precaution remove batteries from the front door bell, or have someone on hand to intercept visitors.

When doing phone interviews, turn your back on anyone else around. Some people will think it funny and try to make you 'corpse' (collapse into giggles) by pulling funny faces or making gestures.

Always remember with a phone interview you have more control than with any other interview. If the worst comes to the worst you can cut the line in mid-conversation claiming a faulty line!

CAN YOU GET ON TV?

Television is a great PR vehicle because viewers do not need to make an effort to watch it. The spread of regular local magazine and news programmes also means that even for small companies and organisations an appearance on the box is now a real possibility. Even if you live in rural Sticksville, don't despair. Local television companies often want to get away from yet another big town story and cover those in the countryside.

Whether you get onto television depends first on if your story is newsworthy or whether it is visual enough. Television deals in pictures so the more you can provide the better.

How to be interviewed on television

If you have the opportunity to appear on television you'll either be interviewed on location or in the studio. Whichever, don't worry about making a fool of yourself. How many people have you ever seen become gibbering idiots on television? Very few. You'll handle it. Only if you're a crook or politician are you likely to come under the kind of severe pressure intended to make you look like an idiot.

Your television 'look'

Make sure your clothing looks good and is appropriate for the subject you're to talk about. Men in particular should be wary of jackets riding up around their neck. The Hunchback of Notre Dame look isn't in this season. Sit on jacket tails as a precaution.

Be prepared

For any television interview, general interview rules still apply, but with a couple of additions. Before the interview begins you'll be asked for some background on the topic. Don't be too eager to please and blurt out everything you know about the subject. Hold something back, otherwise you could find that the presenter's questions are a neat summary of your position, so stealing your thunder.

The interview itself

When the interview begins, look at the interviewer. Don't be distracted by the camera or anything going on elsewhere.

Speak clearly, quite slowly, and concisely. Don't gabble and try not to 'um' or 'ah' since it will make you sound indecisive. If you relax your body, you will relax your voice too. Be sincere and enthusiastic, since the electronic nature of television and radio tends to reduce the impact of your words and therefore their content.

If you 'talk' with your hands, attempt some degree of control over them. A little movement is fine, but doing your impression of a Dutch windmill in a gale force wind isn't. On television any overly emphasised gesticulation or habit is a distraction and irritation for the viewer.

Like their radio cousins television interviews can be done anywhere. To benefit most from them prepare the location before the TV crew arrives, if appropriate. And think in pictures, look for a location that gives the television good shots. If you want the interview to take place in a certain location, then try and make other locations unsuitable or off limits to the camera. Also if appropriate, try to ensure that some of your promotional signs or materials appear discreetly in shot. But don't go over the top. A broadcast journalist will let you promote yourself so far, but if they feel they're being taken on a one-way promotional ride they'll get off the bus.

How to deal with the studio interview

These are more formal than location interviews. They could also mean you're in for a harder time, so you will doubly need to ensure you're as calm and collected as possible for the interview.

So arrive in plenty of time and let them know at reception you've arrived. A researcher or assistant will take you to the hospitality room to wait. Once there, don't overdo the hospitality and avoid alcoholic drinks. Even one wee dram dulls the senses and can give you cottonmouth, making you stumble over the simplest of words, just like certain world famous actors who appear on chatshows.

When the time comes you'll be taken down to the studio. Now the adrenaline will really begin to flow, along perhaps with other things. So make sure you know where the nearest toilet is. This knowledge can be magnificently reassuring.

Your appearance on television
Since your appearance is important for any television interview, your clothing should not only look good but be appropriate. Formal business suits, smart jackets and trousers or skirts are fine. But whatever you wear it shouldn't be too hot or constricting. Television studios are very warm places and you don't want to look as though you're melting... or having your goose cooked. Naturally heavy perspirers should ask the make up department to help them out with a little cosmetic magic. If you undo your collar before the interview, make sure it's done up before you go on air. And should you have come a long way to the studio, especially on a hot day, then take a clean pressed shirt or blouse with you to change into.

Don't wear badges on your jacket lapels or blouses, and avoid peculiar patterned shirts or loud ties. They may look smart to you but they distract the viewer.

The right body language for television
Sit forward in your chair and look alert. Don't lean back, or you'll appear too relaxed and be taken less seriously. At the end of the interview remain seated. The camera is probably still running even if not on you. Wait for the interviewer or the floor manager to indicate that you can now get up.

Even if you are the happiest person in the world, try to restrict your smiling while being interviewed. Do so only slightly. Cheshire Cat grins make you look smug and even arrogant. If the interview is being recorded you even have the possibility of the tape being edited (deliberately or accidentally) in such a way that you are seen smiling at just the wrong moment.

Always listen to what the interviewer is asking and take your time answering questions. Try not to use notes as they look messy. If you need them use a few small index cards. As you answer, don't screw up your face in worry, anger or frustration at the question, or let your breath out with a self satisfied smirk after answering a difficult question. You may still be on camera.

You may also find yourself in opposition to others who oppose your views. If that's the case please avoid getting into a steaming argument with them. This is the time for calmly putting forward your arguments and letting others lose their cool.

HOW TO DEAL WITH THE HOSTILE INTERVIEW

Most radio and television interviews are conducted in good spirit since the interviewer usually has no interest in putting the pressure on. However, there are times when the gloves come off. This is most likely to occur when your organisation is involved in an accident or tragedy, or if you make a decision that is seen as controversial or considered unjust.

Prepare carefully

For the hostile interview you will certainly need your wits about you and preparation is even more important. Find out what areas the interviewer wants to cover when you arrive at the studio; make sure that you aren't steered into areas that you don't want to talk about during the interview.

Prepare the points that you want to make prior to the interview. Have a maximum of three. These are your anchors. Whenever you feel the questioning is sailing into rough waters go back to these points reiterating them time and time again. Be like a broken record. It's important to remember that the interviewer has only limited time to spend attacking you, if you keep stonewalling he's going to create a pretty boring interview unless he moves on. And don't make your answer a hostage to fortune by going off at a tangent, and presenting the interviewer with new directions to follow.

Speak up for yourself

Never let the interviewer put words in your mouth. If you don't think that way then say so. If an incorrect statement that affects you is made by the interviewer or anyone else, correct it immediately. Don't allow the interviewer to jump in before you have finished your answer. If the interviewer sums up your views make sure he or she does so correctly. If they don't, say so and give the correct summary. If a wrong statement is made interrupt and state your case, even though you are off camera. And be alert for a favourite interviewer's trick – making an incorrect statement and then moving quickly on to another subject. Watch out for this right at the end of the programme when the camera stays on the interviewer.

Put your point of view across

Always try to think offensively not defensively. The interview is the opportunity for you to put your side of the story too. Be positive in your statements and avoid phrases such as I think or I believe. That may be true, but your case will be stronger if you state your opinions as though they were facts.

Try not to be too paranoid by thinking the interviewer is out to get you all the time, even if they are. Your paranoia will show and you will appear overly defensive.

Agree film clips in advance
Ask to see any film that may be used before the interview begins. If you are not allowed to see it, then make it clear on air that you have not seen it.

Avoid familiar terms
Be careful about calling the interviewer by name. It makes you look too chummy and suggests that you may be trying to get into their good books.

Avoid jargon
Avoid using jargon and too many technical terms. This makes it look as though you are trying to confuse people, hide behind a smokescreen of words or worse still talk down to them.

Avoid undue emotion
If someone uses an emotive word, don't reinforce it by using it yourself. Make the point in your own way.

Do not enter a pregnant pause
Beware of the interviewer leaving pregnant pauses which you are expected to fill. These are likely to happen after you have made a point which the interviewer wants to draw you on further. After you've said what you want to say, shut up. The interviewer will not be able to allow the pause to go on for too long, that's not good radio or TV.

Have a fallback point
If you can't think of anything to say, go back to a prepared point or stall ('that's an interesting question') then think fast. If in doubt go back to a prepared point even though you have made it before. The interviewer then has the choice of either accepting this as your answer, or asking the question again.

Be accurate
Be as accurate as possible in all you say. Interviewers, especially television ones, may have done their research well and will leap on an inaccuracy. Good preparation is never more important than when you're going to come under attack.

Be calm
Especially in hostile interviews don't wear your emotions or frustrations on your sleeve. The viewing or listening audience may also think the interviewer an idiot, but you must be professional. Likewise witty repostes may make you feel better, but can backfire if you irritate the journalist, especially dangerous if the interview is recorded since you have no control over how it is edited.

HOW TO COPE WITH DOORSTEPPING

One particular version of the hostile interview is the doorstep interview or 'doorstepping', when a journalist or journalists turn up unannounced on the doorstep of your home or place of work. This is most likely to occur if you have been, or are, involved in a major news story, particularly if it is scandalous. If you do fall victim then remember:

- remain cool and as calm as possible. Show that you are in control, you won't give that impression if you appear flustered and living on your nerves;

- be as pleasant as you possibly can. If television cameras are on you then this strategy can help you earn the sympathy of the viewer;

- think carefully before speaking and don't throw lines to the journalist just because they have irritated you;

- decide what you want to say to the accumulated journalistic hordes before you go out to meet them. If you don't want to say anything, then just nod to them, or say 'hello' or 'good morning';

- if you want to speak, stop and say what you have to. Never keep walking and talking. When you have finished walk away briskly;

- always look your best. Denying allegations of incompetence can be difficult when it looks as though you've spent the last three nights asleep in the gutter. Dress well, look smart.

POINTS TO PRACTISE

1. On television, study how politicians ease themselves out of tight corners. Write down some of the phrases they use to extricate themselves ....
   ....
   ....

....
....
....

At the same time watch the professional interviewers. What tricks and methods do they use? Is there a pattern to the interview? It's worth studying the very best interviewers, because their techniques could influence even those in local radio.

2. What are the worst questions that could be asked about a potential business disaster, or controversial topic that you might be involved in? Write them here ....
....
....
....
....
....

Think of the potential answers to the above ....
....
....
....
....
....
....
....
....

Get someone to play the role of the interviewer and put you under pressure. Don't think of this as a game. Play it for real.

3. Identify programmes you would like to appear on, particularly special interest ones which are appealing to your market. The morning or afternoon general interest programmes are always looking to fill air time, and the stories don't even have to be that 'hot' to appear. Early evening regional programmes are good bets with some of the presenters often more than willing to enter into the spirit of things. Look through the *Radio Times* or other listings magazines to identify potential programmes of interest. What programmes do you wish to appear on?
....
....
....
....
....

HOW TO COMPLAIN

An interview, whether on television or radio may be firm, but should also be fair. If you don't think it has been, then you have the right to complain. If you have a complaint about an ITV or Channel 4 programme then complain to the IBA (Independent Broadcasting Association), contact the BBC directly about their programmes. Talk to the producer first. If you receive no satisfaction from them, then contact the Broadcasting Complaints Commission.

USING RADIO PHONE-IN PROGRAMMES

You may not have been personally invited on the air, but radio phone-ins give you the opportunity to barge on anyway. They can be a very useful means of reaching both a local and national audience. Most radio stations hold them on a regular basis, such as Radio 4's *Call Nick Ross*.

If you phone in, work out what you're going to say beforehand and think your arguments through. Then you aren't left floundering if you are asked follow up questions by the presenter.

Since you are unlikely to get through first time, have the show's phone number programmed in to your phone (or hit re-dial). Remember to turn off your radio when phoning otherwise you'll get a nasty electronic howling.

When you do get on air, briefly state the point you want to cover or make, give your name (including your organisation or company name) and your interest in the subject, but don't oversell yourself.

Also, decide when you are going to phone in. Callers at the beginning of the programme set the agenda for it; those in the middle can develop the earlier arguments and take the issues on; while those at the end can summarise the situation.

GETTING ON TO TV DISCUSSION PROGRAMMES

These are the television equivalent of radio's phone-ins, with a participating audience and perhaps a panel of experts or other interested parties. If you are invited to take part and debate an issue, think carefully about accepting. Some of the shows are little more than a free for all, with people shouting at each other as emotions run high. In this atmosphere your points and arguments can be lost in a torrent of abuse. It's difficult to look good or sound professional under these circumstances.

GETTING MEDIA TRAINING

A number of media training courses to help you to improve your interview techniques and media presentation are available, usually run by ex-broadcast journalists. These are especially useful if you want to handle media interest in a particular project, such as the launch of a new product, or event. These courses will help you refine your key messages, then put you through a series of mock interviews of differing intensities. Your efforts will be videoed so you can assess your performance. Such courses are advertised in national newspapers, such as *The Guardian*'s Media Pages on Mondays.

PR IDEAS FOR PROGRAMMES

Television and radio are both insatiable users of material. They are constantly searching for new opportunities to replenish their store of programme ideas. So, if you think your event, company or organisation has an angle to it that would suit the broadcast media, you can either put the idea forward to an independent production company, or to the television companies themselves.

Action tip
What ideas could be developed about your area of activity for a television programme?

1 ....

2 ....

3 ....

4 ....

For further information check out *The Writer's Handbook* and *The Writers' and Artists' Yearbook* which give listings of TV companies and production companies. Look through television listings magazines for programmes that might be suitable for your idea. The chances are that the current series will already have been completed, but your idea might be suitable for the next series.

Action tip
What programmes would be suitable for your programme ideas?

1 ....

2 ....

3 ....

4 ....

If you appear on television or in the media try to be prepared for the increased interest that may result, otherwise you could find yourself with some bad PR on your hands if you can't cope, or provide the service expected.

Case history: Thomas blows it

The owner of a property company, Thomas, is full of his own self importance and confidence. When he is invited on to a regional television programme to be interviewed about a grandiose and controversial plan to develop part of a historic market town, he's delighted.

Always something of a performer who likes to 'wing it' Thomas didn't do any preparation for the interview, nor did he give any thought to how he will come over on television. Thomas gives the interview his all, but instead of coming over as a professional businessman who understands the concerns of others, he creates the image of someone who is going to ride roughshod over all those who disagree with him. He's loud, brash and – worst of all – manoeuvres himself into several corners by saying too much, and ending up defending himself. Not at all the sort of thing he wanted. Of course, Thomas would never consider that his TV appearance had been a factor when his plans were turned down.

So remember, whenever you go on television in particular, think of the image that you want to portray. Then consider your clothes and behaviour as well as content of your words. Examine each closely: do they contribute to the way you want to be seen by others or go against it?

8
Using Newsletters for PR

'It is a great nuisance that knowledge can only be acquired by hard work. It would be fine if we could swallow the powder of profitable information made palatable by the jam of fiction.' W. Somerset Maugham.

Although media relations, that is talking to the press, will play a great part in your public relations efforts, there are other routes you can explore with great success and effectiveness. In the next couple of chapters we will look at two of them: the newsletter and the survey.

WHAT IS A NEWSLETTER?

A newsletter is your organisation's own personal publication. Through it you can keep customers, potential clients, suppliers, decision makers, the local community and the world at large informed about your activities.

They are highly flexible information vehicles and can be used to convey product developments, news, issues, fund raising initiatives. Initially expensive to set up, they can provide a very good cost effective alternative to standard brochures, through the high number of responses they can generate. You can ask people to respond to stories and use these as contact names.

The benefits of newsletters
A well produced and written newsletter has a number of substantial benefits for its publisher.

An air of independence
First, newsletters have a feeling of independence about them so they are treated with less cynicism and scepticism than more obvious promotional devices. To really exploit this advantage a good newsletter should not continually promote your own selfish interests but offer knowledge that people will want to read.

Specialised information
Second, newsletters can be quite specialised, containing information not found elsewhere. Again this provides another reason for people to read and keep them. You can add long term value to your newsletter by punching holes in its left margin so that it can be stored in a ring binder, which you could provide, suitably customised. This keeps your name prominently displayed on a client's shelves and not stuffed away in a filing cabinet.

Newsletters are read more fully
Third, people read newsletters in a way they don't read brochures. While a brochure has to land on the right peron's desk at the right time (when your services are needed) a newsletter can hang around often for months at a time, just biding its time.

Less competition
Fourth, there's less competition from competing newsletters because there are relatively fewer of them around. Brochures on the other hand have to compete against many other brochures. Newsletters therefore tend to stand out.

Attractive to more influential readers
Fifth, newsletters are more likely to get before decision makers' eyes because secretaries are less likely to see newsletters as advertising which they'll throw away.

Income generation
And sixth, though newsletters can be supplied free of charge they can also generate income for you, with readers either taking out a subscription to it, or paying for each issue. Selling advertising space, offering readers services and using grants will also help cover the production costs.

The disadvantages of newsletters
Newsletters however are not without their downside.

- They are inevitably quite expensive to produce, especially if you want one that emphasises quality.

- They also take time and effort, either your's or someone else's to produce.

- And while the idea of a newsletter may be greeted with initial enthusiasm by others, it is likely to prove increasingly difficult to obtain good stories from others, unless they can be motivated to contribute.

CREATING THE RIGHT CONTENT AND STYLE

Anything that goes into a newsletter should be valuable and interesting to the reader, which means that you should really make a decision about who you want your newsletters to be read by: people inside the company, or those outside it.

A major error is to think a newsletter can be everything to everyone and to fill its pages full of information that is of no interest. If it is to be customer-orientated then it should help them solve problems and improve their business or lives; if aimed at staff then it should keep them involved with what is going on in the business and make them feel 'part of the family' by providing detail about who is doing what, when and where. It is a mistake for a single newsletter to try and do both, though many attempt to.

Creating the right image

The newsletter should be written and produced in a way that ties in with the image of your organisation and which appeals to its potential readership. For example, an architectural practice consultant would need to produce a high quality, full colour newsletter on good glossy paper with photographs. However, that could be seen as too lavish for a charity, who would be better off producing a non-nonsense mono publication, probably just with black type on a coloured, recycled paper and no photographs.

Choosing the right format

Newsletters come in all shapes and sizes, each with their own advantages and problems. They can range from A5 through to broadsheet (used by quality daily newspapers such as *The Daily Telegraph* or *The Times*) with the most common size for a newsletter being A4. This is easy to handle and read, and slips happily into envelopes and briefcases.

Newsletters smaller than this can be regarded with less respect, while the more you make your newsletter look like a newspaper in terms of size and style, the more people will think that it contains news.

Newsletters should be long enough to do their intended job which means they can range from just one sheet to multi-paged mini magazines. When just starting a newsletter, don't be too ambitious. You may think you can fill sixteen pages with no trouble at all, but can you? And can you keep on doing this edition after edition? It's better to start off slowly, find out what interest there is in the newsletter then build on that.

Using colour
A black and white publication is cheaper to produce than a coloured counterpart, though it can lack visual impact. A single 'spot' colour used on the front cover helps add to the attraction while keeping costs down.

Using illustrations
Photographs and illustrations add to production costs but give a huge visual lift. Black and white shots are cheaper to produce than colour. You can reach an effective compromise by using colour pictures on the front cover, while keeping the inner pages black and white.

WRITING AND EDITING NEWSLETTERS

Whatever its function or purpose, someone has to take responsibility for writing and editing the newsletter. This entails deciding what is to go into the newsletter, finding interesting story ideas, writing original stories, editing the work of others and if necessary briefing photographers. It will also be necessary to work with a designer on the layout and look of the newsletter.

If no one in your organisation has these writing or editing skills then you'll need to employ someone, probably a professional writer or editor, to do it.

How to find an editor or writers
- Advertise for them in professional magazines such as the *UK Press Gazette*, or writing magazines such as *Writers News*.

- Approach a local journalist or writer. A journalist on the local paper may be able to do some or even all of the work for you, if your newsletter is infrequent or can be put together quickly.

- Contact the British Association of Industrial Editors (BAIE) and ask them for help and advice.

- Approach a local public relations consultant or company to take on the task. This is probably the most expensive option and one the consultancy may not want to take on unless it's part of a larger PR campaign.

- Contact the author of this book, who has successfully edited and produced newsletters and corporate words for organisations that include tourist boards, distillers, chemical, electronics and computer companies, airports and dairies.

ORGANISING NEWSLETTER DESIGN AND PRINT

Do-it-yourself newsletter design is only to be recommended if you have competent design or DTP skills. Shoddy and amateur looking newsletters reflect badly on your organisation, especially if you are a business or commercial concern. If you are intending to design your own newsletter, then take the time to get good training, preferably as much hands on experience as possible, and read books on newsletter and magazine design. Designers can be found in the *Creative Handbook* or the *Yellow Pages*.

As a cost effective, but somewhat riskier approach, contact your local art college, talk to the tutors and find out if they have graphic design students who are capable of taking on the job. Some printers have an in-house design facility that can help you. For more detailed information on practical newsletter production read Graham Jones's *How to Publish a Newsletter* (How To Books, 2nd edition 1995).

HOW TO DISTRIBUTE YOUR NEWSLETTER

Newsletters can be sent out to a regular list of staff, clients, potential customers, suppliers and opinion formers or be left at pick-up points where would-be customers or suppliers (or anyone interested) can pick up a copy. Reception areas, libraries and tourist information places are all the types of places where newsletters and similar publications can be left.

Using a mailing list

You will probably have a mailing list already of existing clients to whom you can send your newsletter, but you might like to extend potential readership by using a bought in mailing list to reach new clients.

These lists can be bought from **list brokers**. Usually you will be expected to rent a minimum number of names and addresses, which can be supplied to you on computer disk or more likely on adhesive labels.

You will only be able to use the names once and just to make sure you do, the list will be 'salted' with false names to catch you out. The charge is usually per 1,000 names and addresses (eg £100 per 1,000)

YOUR NEWSLETTER CHECKLIST

Decide the purpose of your newsletter, this will determine the information that it needs to contain. Write that purpose down here:

....

....

....

....

Who is your newsletter to be aimed at? People outside your organisation or within it? Again this will determine the content. List your potential readerships here:

....

....

....

....

How many times a year will you publish your newsletter?

....

....

How many pages will it have?

....

Will it be colour or black and white?

....

Will it be supplied free, have a cover price, or be available by subscription?

....

Where will you gather the information from?

....

....

....

Who will do that research?

....

Who will do the writing?

....

Who will do the editing?

....

Who will do the research?

....

Who will do the interviewing?

....

Will you need additional equipment and other resources to produce your newsletter?

....

Will you need extra training (writing, DTP)?

....

How will you promote the newsletter?

....

....

....

Case history: Andrea's accountancy newsletter

An accountancy firm has for some years produced a newsletter for its clients. Standard taxation and fiscal matters are covered, with copy and ideas supplied by the firm's staff. But Andrea, one of the firm's partners, thinks there is scope for developing the newsletter on a wider basis by going elsewhere for editorial.

With that in mind she contacted people outside the firm, figures in industry and the accountancy profession, and asked if they would be interviewed for the newsletter. The response was good because Andrea approached them as the publisher and editor of the newsletter; after all it was also good PR for the interviewees.

As soon as the newsletter was published, Andrea sent her interviewees 20–30 copies so they could hand them out to their clients and suppliers. Not only did this do some of the distribution work for Andrea's firm, but it also brought in potential new readers ... and clients.

9
Creating News with a Survey

'I am a monarch of all I survey.' William Cowper.

'Them that asks no questions isn't told a lie'. Rudyard Kipling from *A Smuggler's Song*.

THE POWER OF THE SURVEY

'If in doubt, do a survey.' That's been the cry of many PR consultants and agencies who want to create news. And though a rather hackneyed idea and something of a fall back position, surveys are not without their merits as they do provide a peg on which editors can hang stories. They can also help portray your organisation as important with something worthwhile to say. Indeed, survey results are run frequently by the press themselves and and often make lead news, though they are more likely to be of interest to the national and trade press rather than the locals.

Surveys are a good means of 'manufacturing' news, especially if they generate unexpected or surprising results. However, if the results are too surprising, even unbelievable, then the survey may actually work against you, even if the results are true. This casts doubt on the whole of the survey and of course you and your orgnaisation. You need only look at the opinion polls at General Election time to see how the most carefully conducted surveys can be discredited or ridiculed.

HOW TO CONDUCT A SURVEY

Before you embark on a survey, ask yourself why you want it in the first place.

- What specifically do you hope it will achieve? Perhaps there is another means of obtaining PR which would be better suited to your needs?

- If a survey seems the right idea, how long will it take to complete? Is this going to be a short-term 'snapshot' survey, or something longer term? If the survey needs to be run over a long period of time, do you have the resources to carry it through to conclusion?

- How many people will you need to do the survey and who will they be – you, your staff, or an outside group or company? Even a simple survey undertaken by a professional research group will cost thousands of pounds, though the better known the research company the more credible the survey. As a cost effective solution then you could contact a local college to see if their business studies, maths or psychology students might like to take on the task.

- Next decide who you are going to survey and will you be surveying them at random or to some predetermined pattern? For instance, you could just stop anyone in the street, or only those who meet certain criteria, such as being the right age or sex.

- How many people are you going to ask? The more people you survey the more credibility the results will have. Of course, if there are only 50 people in your total survey population, then polling 40 of them will give your survey a high degree of significance.

- You now know who you are going to survey, but what are you going to ask them? This will depend on what you are trying to achieve. Designing survey questions is something of a skilled task, which can directly affect the results you obtain.

- Finally, what method or methods are you going to employ to survey people? Will you ask questions on a one to one basis in the street; will you ask them at your premises or theirs; will you ask them questions on the phone or by using a postal questionnaire?

DOING A POSTAL SURVEY

A postal questionnaire can help you cut survey costs, espeically if you send it out when you mail other information, statements or bills.

Be brief

Postal questionnaires should be short and ask simple questions. The more difficult you make the questions the lower will be your response rate.

Be relevant

Ask questions that are relevant to the respondents. If they can't see why they should answer the questions then very few questionnaires will be returned. Make the questionnaire as attractive and readable as possible by using plenty of white space on it and giving it a memorable title.

Offer a reason to respond

Also explain in an accompanying letter why you are asking the questions and outline why potential respondents to this survey will benefit from answering them. For instance, they will experience an improved service or speedier response to their enquiries.

Consider offering respondents an incentive to reply. This will put up response rates. Suitable incentives could be small gifts, prize draws or discounts off your services or products. And reassure respondents that the information they provide will be regarded in the strictest confidence. Explain that they don't even have to write their name on the survey.

Enclose a stamped addressed envelope for the reply. You can't expect respondents to pay for your survey.

Be prepared to re-mail

If response rates are poor, re-mail the questionnaire to non-respondents, saying that you assume they didn't receive the original.

DOING A TELEPHONE SURVEY

If speed is important, for instance if you are reacting to a breaking news story, a telephone survey is the answer. Since using the phone is expensive, set a budget for yourself. This will determine the number of calls that can be made and when.

Checklist – who will you call?

Will you call people at random? ....

Will you call people according to some set pattern? If so, what will it be? ....

Are you going to do the calling? (If you aren't, who is?) ....
....

How many people are you going to call? ....

Who will they be?...
....
....

Who will collate the results? ....

Deciding on questions

Keep the questions simple and don't ask many of them. You are using up your client's time and adding to your phone bill. Try not to be on the phone more than 4–5 minutes with each person you survey. Make sure you don't get side tracked into small talk since this can cost you dear in money and time. Consequently don't ad lib. If you need a script then write one up and use it.

Case history: Graham's music survey

His record store was doing fairy well, but Graham Merrick thought he could do with some extra publicity, especially concerning the range of classical music that he carried. He liked the idea of doing a survey, but wasn't sure how he could conduct one that was relevant to his business. After all he was just a small town retailer with only a limited budget.

Then it came to him. What if he used information that he already had in the form of his sales figures to supply the local paper with a chart of the local Top Twenty, both classical and pop?

The newspaper liked the idea and has been running Graham's charts for the last two years. It provides them with local editorial and Graham with PR. This is an idea that could be used by other retailers such as food suppliers and book and video shops.

DISTRIBUTING SURVEY RESULTS

When you've collated the results of your survey, decide what the main results of it are and incorporate these into a press release. Keep more technical details and full survey details for an accompanying backgrounder.

The results should be tailored to meet the needs of the publication they are going to. For instance, trade publications will expect a higher level of tehnical information than a national newspaper, though both may want to cover the story.

If your survey is nationally based, then break it down if you can on a regional basis. This then provides you with a series of additional stories that can be sent out to the regional and local press.

Action tip

Watch the press for other surveys. What gives them their distinctive angle? Why were they undertaken – to reinforce an existing point of view for instance?

POINTS FOR DISCUSSION

1. How might a survey help promote your own organisation?

2. Would a postal or telephone survey be more appropriate to your needs?

3. What questions would you include in your survey, and how many would you have?

4. What would be the cost of doing such a survey, and how could you equate this with the possible benefits?

10
Making Your Voice Heard

THE ADVANTAGES OF SPEAKING IN PUBLIC

Public speaking as a PR tool, 'just saying a few words', is a low key and high quality approach to public relations but one at which many people blanche. But these reservations should be overcome because there are substantial benefits.

The key benefits

- It helps promote you as an expert in your field. This is equally important at a local, regional or national level.

- It develops awareness of your company, group or cause.

- It offers you the opportunity to obtain feedback from people you do business with.

- It helps generate sales and business leads.

- It's a good means of networking with potential contacts.

- It generates follow up opportunities to speak to other interested groups.

- It's cost effective. You don't pay to make speeches and very often it can actually earn you money. Many make a substantial living from public speaking.

WHO TO SPEAK TO

Public speaking only works to your PR advantage if you talk to the right people, so you need to decide upon your target audience. For example, if you are an architect you might want to talk to builders, contractors, planning officers and fellow architects. As a personal insurance adviser you would be willing to talk about financial planning to virtually any general interest group you could put yourself in front of.

Groups regularly wanting speakers

Having decided who to talk to, you'll need to make contact with them. Special interest groups, business clubs, or sports clubs, to name but a few, will all have regular meetings where speakers can be heard. Local associations, organisations, groups, WIs, tourist associations, business groups, sports teams, hobby groups, church groups and many others are constantly on the look out for speakers to talk to members. Find out their addresses or phone numbers and call up the secretaries with the suggestion that you talk to their members on your subject.

Do your background research

You know who you want to talk to and where to find them, and now you have to decide not only what you are going to say to them but also what they want to hear. To do this effectively you will need to do background research. The organiser of the talk, generally the secretary of the association or group, should be able to tell you much of what you know, though do not be surprised if now and then what you are told proves to be hopelessly inaccurate. If that turns out to be so, then always be prepared to adapt your speech accordingly, especially if you begin to feel you are talking down to your audience.

This is some of the information you must obtain from organisers, if you want to be a well received public speaker:

- Who will be in the audience and how many of them will there be?

- What will be their interests?

- Will they be male or female, and of what age?

- What attitudes will they have, about your subject and the world in general? Are they hostile to certain subjects and enthusiastic about others, and if so what are they?

- Are there issues that are particularly troubling them at the moment?

- How much do they know about the subject? If they know little then your talk will be different from if they were experts.

- Has the audience listened to a similar talk recently?

- How long will you be expected to talk?

- Will there be a question and answer session afterwards?

- And will there by a PA (public address) system to amplify your voice?

WHAT TO SAY?

Speeches given for PR purposes are really no different from any other type of speech. There is nothing magical or mystical about them. And like any other speech they require thought, planning and good presentation if they are to be carried off well and successfully.

Be interesting

It should be obvious that your speech should be of interest and relevance to the group you're talking to. If not, they'll be bored, and you'll be thought boring and the PR value of your talk will be of less value than a single Green Shield stamp.

Budget your time

Mostly you will be expected to talk for 20–30 minutes at lunchtime and probably 40–45 minutes in the evening, with some time taken at the end, probably about 10–15 minutes for questions. Don't attempt to talk for longer than this unless you are a talented speaker (but make sure someone else tells you that, rather than just convincing yourself you are). In any case you will rarely need to speak for longer unless there is a specific reason to put across a great deal of information.

Be entertaining

Make your talk as rewarding and entertaining as possible for the audience. Visual aids can be highly valuable in making your speech memorable. Slide projectors, blackboards, flipcharts, whiteboards, overhead projectors, videos and film strips all have their advantages. But whatever you use make sure you can operate it properly; your audience doesn't want to watch your efforts to learn.

Even though you are in front of a captive audience, you shouldn't abuse the opportunity by banging on about how wonderful you and your business or organisation are (unless of course that is what you have been specifically asked to do). People don't like listening to big heads. It bores them.

Always remember that the content of your speech should be of interest to your audience, so think about *them* and what *they* want, then give it to them. They'll love you for it.

A warning word
Don't ever be tempted to tell risqué or blue jokes. This will do nothing for your professional credibility and is bound to offend some in the audience. Jokes do have their place in public speaking, but not everyone will share your sense of humour.

How to develop your speech
Deciding the key points
On a sheet of paper write down the subject of your talk. Beneath this list every point related to this subject, which may be twenty or more points. Now decide which of these points you really want to get over to the audience. Choose three at the most which ideally should be related to one another. Then develop each of these points with sub-points that support your main points.

Creating a logical order
With this done put these points into logical order so that one flows on to the next. Your talk should have a structure that begins with an introduction. In this you will tell your audience what you are going to talk about, and perhaps why you are going to talk about the subject in this way. Next you have the meat of your argument, in which you deal first with point one, then two, and then three. Finally, conclude the talk by running back over the points you've already made.

Drafting the speech
When you have done all this, write out the speech in full making it as lively and interesting as possible. Don't over-use facts and figures. Use anecdotes wherever possible. Keep sentences short and simple; don't use long and complicated words you might stumble over. Do a number of drafts until you are happy with the result.

This writing process is an important one, because while doing it you will become more conversant with the subject matter. With this done, begin highlighting all the main points and the sub-points and the phrases that remind you about them. By the time you finish you should have an aide memoire for your talk with the single words or phrases.

Your final notes
Write your notes down on white index cards, a few notes on each one.

Number each card so that if you drop them you can put them in order quickly.

PREPARING TO SPEAK

Practice makes perfect

You can't expect to just stand up and make a good speech so begin rehearsing early. Don't try to remember the exact words you've used previously. Use the single words and phrases on the index card to trigger your thoughts. By doing this, rather than reading from a script, your talk will be more relaxed and natural and the audience won't have to look at the top of your head, which happens if you read.

Take every opportunity to speak in front of others, no matter how many. If you are very nervous about standing and 'spouting off' in front of people, start slowly. When you're with friends in the pub, clubs, restaurant and at home with friends then make an additional effort to hold the floor longer than you normally would. This may be just a couple of minutes at first, but can be built up. In this environment you will feel more confident and comfortable, your nerves will diminish and you will improve your performance.

Alternatively, check your local training and education colleges for public speaking courses. Each student learns about the techniques of speaking and then has to write and deliver a series of speeches. Short at first, but growing longer. Their efforts are then assessed by the tutor and the others.

Delivering your speech

Try to keep a relaxed stance when speech making. Stand with your feet comfortably apart. Hands are always a problem; they can either rest comfortably on the lectern or table in front of you or be kept in jacket pockets. Don't cross your arms in front of you as this makes you look defensive. If you normally use your hands to make a point then do so, but within reason; you don't want to look like a flailing octopus. Think in terms of giving a little talk to people, not a speech, which sounds impossibly formal.

Maintaining eye contact with your audience will help hold their interest. One advantage of using notes, which you should look at as briefly as possible, is that you will be able to watch your audience. So cast your eyes around, look at various sections for three or four seconds at a time, before passing on to a new area. Try to divide the audience into five or six groups, depending on its size. Distribute your glances evenly, don't stare at one particular individual or you will make them uncomfortable.

Case history: Peter fails to prepare

Peter runs a successful accountancy practice and can see a great number of opportunities to talk to special interest groups about financial planning. But Peter is very arrogant; he knows his subject so why does he need to rehearse or practise his delivery? Well of course he doesn't!

Come the day of his first public speaking engagement Peter proceeds to deliver the most catastrophic speech. Immediately on standing up in front of 150 people, his normal confidence makes a run for the door, leaving his mind completely blank. And not having the protection of notes, he has no foundations to fall back on. He stutters, blusters and rambles for fifteen minutes, before sitting down exhausted and humiliated ten minutes prematurely.

Needless to say the audience is not impressed. What they have just seen suggests a man who does not know his subject and who inspires no confidence whatever. Would you trust him with your money?

The moral of this story is simple: if you are going to deliver speeches as part of your public relations strategy, then ensure you are competent otherwise you'll be creating the wrong impression, that reflects badly on you. If you do lack confidence in your public speaking abilities, find speaking opportunities that don't involve talking about your company, organisation or speciality. Then if things don't go well you'll just be seen as someone who can't talk about coin collecting rather than an accountant who doesn't know anything about money.

FOLLOWING UP YOUR TALK

Once the final word of wisdom has fallen from your lips do some networking. After all, you are the star of the show and people will want to talk with you, whether to agree or disagree with what you've just said. Remember, you'll be seen as something of an expert so use that authority when you speak with potential customers and suppliers.

Leave some information about yourself at the venue. This can be a simple leaflet or background notes about your talk, but it should always carry your name, address and contact number so that people who don't get to speak with you can make a follow up. These handouts are best left simple, a single sheet of folded A4 is enough, avoid large brochures, which people have to hang on to all through an evening and can't be slipped into a jacket pocket.

Reasons why you might turn down a speech

Sometimes it isn't appropriate or necessary to make a speech. You might wish to turn down the opportunity when:

- it will take too long to research and write the speech;

- it won't lead to other opportunities;

- you can make a more profitable speech elsewhere on the same night;

- not enough of the right people will hear your speech to warrant the effort;

- or there are others on the bill who you don't want to speak against.

How to develop your public speaking career

With a successful talk under your belt you have two options: to repeat the same speech to a similar interest group, or to develop other speeches which you can give to different audiences. This second route is best, since it gives you confidence that you really are a public speaker, while at the same time offering you more opportunities to promote yourself.

Joining the lecture circuit

Once you have developed confidence in your public speaking abilities, you might consider the lecture circuit, touring the country (or world) making speeches to invited and paying audiences. This is a great form of personal public relations since it raises your profile, costs you little and can earn you very good money. Speaking fees can run from hundreds to many thousands of pounds per engagement. And there are many chances to speak. One estimate suggests that there are 4,000 opportunities in the UK every week!

If you want to get onto the lecture circuit contact special interest groups and secretaries of associations. The *Directory of British Associations* and *Councils, Committees and Boards* both published by CBD Research should be available in the reference section of your local library. These give useful contact names, addresses and background information.

Draw up a list of those you are interested in and write to the secretaries. Say why you think you have something of interest to say to their association's members; why you have something that's different to say; how long you would be willing to speak for; where you would be prepared to speak; and what would be your fee and other considerations, such as travelling expenses. Also give background about yourself, including your public speaking experience.

Be prepared to serve out a speaking 'apprenticeship', not asking for too much too soon. But, even in the early days of your speaking career consider yourself a professional and always ask for a fee, though you'll greatly increase your chances of securing a speaking opportunity if you make it clear to the organiser that under normal circumstances you would charge £300 but because you consider this to be a worthwhile cause, you'll donate the fee back to the organisation and won't submit an invoice.

Action tip

Draw up a list of local organisations, perhaps work related or even to do with a hobby of pastime, to which you feel you could have something to say.

Organisation   *Speaking topic*

....

....

....

....

Contact a few of the above organisations and explain that you would like to talk to them. If you are new to public speaking then approach those that you least want to influence or impress. Use them and their members as guinea pigs and a means of improving your speaking performance. When you are a more experienced and confident speaker you can then start approaching the groups you do want to influence.

PUTTING ON SEMINARS

So far in this chapter we've looked at ways to exploit existing public speaking opportunities, but how about creating them for yourself?

One of the best ways of doing this is by organising a seminar, a teaching session for people who want to learn more about your particular subject or activity. Seminars are especially useful in areas where information changes frequently, as in financial services and computing.

Seminars are a great opportunity for excellent market research and to obtain feedback about what you have said from your audience. And, if you give people who attend your seminars value for money and a good time then they will be more than happy and your company will benefit accordingly from the good PR.

Seminars are not suitable for all businesses. For instance, it would be difficult to see how a fruit and vegetable shop would benefit from one, though it might be worth it for a flower shop if they supply blooms for a flower arranging seminar.

Checklist – would a seminar work for you?

Yes   *No*

1. Does your area of activity or interest change rapidly? (If so, then people will want up to the minute information. A seminar can provide them with it.)   ____   ____

2. Will your seminar help the potential audience make money, save money, improve their personal fortunes, or feel happier about their lives?   ____   ____

3. Is there a topical interest in your subject? (If it seen as being rather old fashioned then not many people will want to come along.)   ____   ____

4. Will enough people be interested in the subject of your seminar? (If your theme is too narrow then again you won't attract the interest.)   ____   ____

5. Do you have a means of telling your potential audience about your seminar? (If there isn't a publication that covers your special area of interest, or if it's difficult to obtain a mailing list of prospective attendees, then it may well be difficult to attract interest in the seminar.)   ____   ____

6. Seminars take up a lot of time so you will need to have the resources available to ensure their success. (Your seminar had better be good otherwise it will reflect very badly on you.)   ____   ____

How to organise a seminar

You will have to begin organising a seminar in plenty of time, because it will require a great deal of effort and hard work.

The venue
First, choose a venue. This could be on your company premises, though a better solution would be a hotel function room, which must be large enough for the number of people you expect. Seminars should be held at good venues, otherwise it will reflect badly on you. You will normally be expected to supply food and drinks so make sure these can be supplied.

Setting the fee
Second, seminars can either be free or charged for (they can often generate a sizeable income). Indeed, charging a fee can enhance the professional standing of your seminar by increasing its perceived value, though it will reduce the number of people likely to attend although their quality may well rise.

Promotion
Third, begin promoting the event as soon as you have finalised basic information about the venue and speakers. This you can do through public relations (a press release to relevant publications and programmes), advertising, direct mail or telemarketing. Telemarketing can be a particularly good means of pulling in attendees late in the day, especially if they have already been mailed with information about the seminar.

Finalising the numbers
Fourth, try to finalise the numbers of attendees as far in advance as possible. Set a closing date for responses, probably 4–6 weeks beforehand. This will give you sufficient time to assess the level of interest and do extra promotion if required. If interest in the seminar is so great that you could fill the venue several times over, then operate on a first come first served basis, and offer those unsuccessful the same seminar on another date.

Preparing the work materials
Fifth, create the work materials, if any, your attendees will require or find useful for the seminar. These materials need not be complex and can range from a simple work book, to illustrated documents and binders.

Case history: the accountants' Budget seminar

Each year immediately after the Budget, accountants Chappell, Peacock, Henderson and Crow hold a seminar on what fiscal and tax changes will mean to their clients and local businesses.

But this is a seminar with a difference, because they turn it into an event. And each year they give it a different theme into which Budget news is interwoven. One year their seminar was set in Ancient Egypt, another time in outer space. They hire a local theatre and use their sets and costumes. Of course, the preparatory work is done long before the Budget so only the new details have to be added in. The accountants even create a number of scenarios to cover all eventualities.

After five or six years of doing this, the Budget show really has a strong following, with perhaps 300 people attending. From a PR point this is a memorable seminar and each year they pick up a lot of press coverage and business from it.

POINTS FOR DISCUSSION

1. What would it take for you to become an effective and regular public speaker? What practice and help would you need?

2. Give three examples of how good public speaking skills could help you promote our own organisation in new ways.

3. Draw up a plan for a series of seminars designed to attract and help your clients or customers.

11
Meeting the Press

So far we have discussed how to connect with individual members of the press and media, but there are times when it is better to meet the press en masse, saving much time and effort. The two most accepted means of doing this are through

- press conferences

- facility trips.

GIVING A PRESS CONFERENCE

What is a press conference?
A press conference is really the physical equivalent of a press release with journalists called together, then in a speech or speeches told the what, when, where, why, who and how of the story.

Like press releases, press conferences should be as short as possible, get to the point and reveal their purpose very quickly. There should be an obvious emphasis on news. Background information should be given briefly and only as necessary to set the scene. Backgrounders can be supplied to answer any obvious follow up questions journalists may have.

Press conferences are best suited to hard news that has national or at least good local impact. You are therefore most likely to use them when:
- launching a new product or service
- announcing a major improvement to an old product
- highlighting a new use for an existing product
- revealing new appointments and promotions
- opening new branches or offices or refurbished old ones
- making award presentations
- announcing new sponsors for charitable events
- announcing new prestigious contracts won
- announcing the breaking of records

- celebrating important anniversaries
- making predictions about the market or industry
- publishing survey results
- revealing that a VIP is to speak or appear at an event
- publishing a controversial book
- quashing a rumour.

When to hold a press conference

The success or failure of your press conference can depend entirely on when it is held. So, try to avoid days when there is a lot of other news about. Of course you can do nothing if disasters occur, but days when there is an obvious news story, such as General Election results, should be avoided.

Mondays and Fridays are generally the clearest and weakest of news days and therefore good ones on which to hold conferences. But again avoid them if they coincide with an obvious big news story.

For widest media coverage, the press conference should begin around 10.30–11.00am. You can then meet the deadlines of evening papers and lunchtime television and radio news.

Using the 'silly season'
The summer 'silly season' is good press conference time, if your news can afford to wait until then. During this period regular news is slack with Parliament not sitting and people away on holiday.

Choosing the conference venue

Though they can be held anywhere, generally company meeting rooms or hotel function rooms are best. Ideally, the venue should be easily accessible and centrally located within town or city centres rather than in a rural location. The quicker the venue is to reach for most journalists the more likely they are to turn up.

The turnout
Don't expect everyone you invite to turn up. You may only get one or two out of ten coming, but make sure the venue is large enough to take 50–60% of the journalists you ask. And too large a venue is better than too small. Parking should be available near the venue, and sufficient.

Reception
Place a small table at the entrance to the venue. On this you can have pre-printed name tags, or a signing-in book. Put **press packs** elsewhere, such as in a reception room, so journalists don't end up carrying something the moment they walk through the door.

The main table
At the front of the room have a table and chairs for speakers and behind this a backdrop made from painted hardboard or something similar. On this can be your logo, name or slogan. It should stand seven feet high approximately, so that nothing of the wall behind can be seen to distract from the speakers.

Technical facilities
If television is invited to the conference, make sure that there are adequate power points for lights and cameras. A side room set aside for private interviews with speakers may be appropriate.

Photographers will often turn up before journalists, so help them do their job by letting them take stock shots before the conference begins.

And, if you are going to release the text of speeches, do so after they've been given. As people can read faster than someone can talk, they'll reach the end before the speech is finished and start to lose interest. Instead, provide just a summary of the speech with the press kit.

Sending out press conference invitations

Invitations and press releases sent out to publicise a press conference should strongly emphasise why the conference is taking place. Invitations should contain all the basic information that a journalist needs to know about the event. Include a map of the venue location if this will be useful. Invitations can be written on standard letterheads. Do not go overboard with scalloped edge or gold trimmed cards. They should be sent to news editors or editors.

The number of invitations you send out will depend upon the importance of your press conference and the number of publications and news outlets that will be interested. A press conference that has great general appeal would be of interest to the dailies, television, the Sundays, the foreign press, freelancers and television and radio, while a more specialised press release would attract only a few journalists from the specialist press.

Case history: Derek checks the numbers

Derek is organising a press conference for his company. After he has sent out the invitations to journalists, he then follows up with a phone call to each publication about a week before the conference to see if the invitations have arrived safely. He doesn't at this stage ask if anyone is coming. This he does in another phone call the day before or on the morning of the press conference itself.

```
The Organisers of the Hedgehog Liberation Society
           invite you to a press conference


    SUBJECT:   Hedgehog Ownership Survey Results

    AT:        The Savoy Hotel, Worcester

    DATE:      28 November 199X

    TIME:      10.00 am



               For further details contact:
               Julian Sonic
               Tel (0171) 123 4567
```

Fig. 9. A simple invitation to a press conference.

By only finding out who is coming at this late stage, Derek is able to obtain a very accurate idea of the numbers that will be coming.

Giving press receptions

These are informal events to which the press and others are invited to hear speeches and see new products. Food and drink is often made available. Receptions are not usually arranged for issuing hard news but are better suited to soft news items such as 'arty' events. Invitations would therefore be sent out to art page editors and newspapers' diarists.

ORGANISING FACILITY TRIPS

If you have a product, or offer a service which you feel would be better written about and promoted if journalists could experience it themselves, then organise a facility trip. Holiday companies do this frequently, picking up the tab for journalists to fly out and enjoy their latest package tour.

Facility trips can be offered either to single journalists or groups of them. Don't make these groups too large, especially if you are bringing them to premises with limited space. Split groups into no more than 10–12 and if you take them on a tour of a factory organise their routes carefully so that you don't get traffic jams.

Leave yourself plenty of time to organise facility trips. You'll want them to be as well thought out as possible to ensure that they go smoothly and don't leave you with egg on your face.

A briefing may be necessary when the journalists arrive and you may need to supply office facilities such as faxes, phones and word processors.

CREATING PRESS KITS (PACKS)

Whether you're organising a press conference, reception or facility trip, you will need to supply the invited journalists with press kits. These can range from just a few pages of paper in a folder to quite thick dossiers, but all have the same purpose, to provide journalists with valuable background and briefing materials.

What to put in a press kit
These can include, where appropriate, any of the following:

- the ubiquitous press release (those already sent out and new ones)

- general background information on the event or conference, details of its history, or the range of other products or services offered by a company

- biographies of key members of staff. These should include place of birth, work experience, published articles, membership of relevant organisations and professional bodies, what they are best known for and winners of which awards

- profiles of speakers at an event giving their biographical details

- a brochure

- photographs of people and products. Ideally these should be 5″ x 7″ black and white shots. Head and shoulder shots are fine for people. All should be captioned

- your business card

- articles and tear sheets from magazines, which help establish your credibility. These can be written either by you or someone else. Always include the date and the title of the publication of each

- a sheet of interesting quotes from relevant personnel. The name of the speaker should be given for each, as well as the context in which it was said if this helps explain the quote

- a calendar of future events if relevant

- technical data sheets

- product samples

- promotional items such as pens, stickers and hats

- a folder that contains the rest of the information. These can be specially made up, or off the shelf. They need to be able to take A4 sheets flat, perhaps with a pouch.

PUTTING ON PR EVENTS

Events can be great ways of generating press attention and for that reason are frequently used. Charities, for instance, use them all the time to help raise awareness about a situation and funds for the cause.

What makes a good PR event?
First, the event must be worthwhile. Otherwise, few people will be interested and it will be ignored by the media. Worse, a poorly thought out event may create a negative impression of your organisation, the very opposite of what you want to achieve. You should have a strong idea of what you want to achieve by putting on the event, and the stories you feed to the press should focus on this.

Staying in charge
You must be able to stay in control of the event and the publicity for it. Someone must take responsibility for handling all of the PR. Don't let several people start talking to the press. Or if they do, then they should let the person who is in charge of PR know immediately. If you don't ensure this then you will find that you are feeding out similar stories, or being contacted by the press who have already spoken to others. You get wires crossed, contradictions occur and the event starts looking as though it is being run by clowns.

Exploiting the opportunities
Ideally the event should be one that can generate lots of different story angles so that it's as productive as possible. Don't just do a sponsored walk, but make it a litter pick at the same time. The litter you collect can then be built into a litter mountain at the end of the walk making for a good photo opportunity.

Prepare early
If you are handling the PR for it, then become involved with the organisation of the event at an early stage. Others may not be so PR aware, and input at the initial stages can be tremendously helpful if you introduce story twists and angles at an early moment. It is far easier then than later.

Ring the changes
If you are publicising an annual event, don't stand still, but think of new story angles each year. What new ideas can you bolt on? Are there local celebrities you can involve? Can you introduce costumes? Can you use an unusual venue or form of transport? Can you link with another event or an anniversary? Can you team up with a publication in a joint promotion of the event? You then get promotion and publicity for it, while the publication is seen to be doing something worthy. It also has a story. Local radio stations are often particularly good in supporting worthy causes.

Always look for new angles to an event, especially if it tends to be run of the mill. For instance, if you are organising a sponsored walk (a rather common event), you could give it a twist by saying that you are going to walk the height of Everest up hills. This means that you might be able to bring in mountaineer celebrities or obtain sponsorship from equipment suppliers and manufacturers.

If you are involved with an event how can you develop more news angles so as to promote it? Write down five new angles.

....

....

....

....

....

Action tip

Can you become involved in a local event that others are organising? Begin by looking through the local papers to see if they are running stories on future events, or look through a 'local event calendar' to see what annual events take place.

Case history: Tony's Alpine weekend

A small Midlands town is twinned with an Austrian equivalent. To celebrate the connection, it wants to hold an Alpine weekend in the autumn. Tony, who is in charge of promoting the event, is looking for the big idea that will capture everyone's imagination locally and hopefully bring in some media coverage which will encourage tourism to the town.

He organises a brain storming session with other members of the organising committee. They come up with everything Austrian they can think of from cowbells to Alpine horns.

Then someone suggests skiing. The town has no ski slope and in October it certainly won't have any snow, but what it does have are hills, in fact the main street drops down at over 30 degrees. So why not build a ski run on it? Now that is a big idea and one that should guarantee local, regional and probably national press interest. And if it's successful once then it could be successful again and again. Tony claps his hands and leaves to find some skiers.

Case history: The Malvern Water Cure Event

In its first year, the Malvern Water Cure Event, which celebrated the 150th anniversary of the town's famous water treatments, was a resounding publicity success. Local, regional and national coverage was achieved in newspapers, while regional television and regional and national radio ran pieces. The publicity was even picked up by an American radio station, which then sold the story on to Canada.

After all that, how could the event be promoted in its second year? Two solutions were found: to move the event on by not just focusing on the water treatment, but bringing in the town's Victorian connections and secondly to recreate one of the Water Cure treatments, the spectacular Descending Douche. This piece of equipment dumped gallons and gallons of water onto a 'patient' beneath. Such a strong visual image caught the imagination of broadcasters and journalists who came along with their cameras and pens.

12
Coping with the Unexpected

'It's a good thing to make mistakes, so long as you're found out quickly.' Attributed to John Maynard Keynes.

Of course, it's always best to prevent problems rather than having to deal with them. But from time to time bad things happen to everyone, no matter how careful you are. And bad PR can arise when you don't offer as good a service as possible, such as failing to deliver on time; when your goods are sub standard; when you don't resolve problems with customers and suppliers quickly enough; if you or your staff are surly and unpleasant to clients or customers; and when you don't keep people informed about things that go wrong, and let them find out from other sources. Just think back to occasions when you have had bad service or food at a restaurant, haven't you told friends about it and warned them not to go there? That's 'small' bad PR but then there is its big brother.

Generally these hiccups will only be minor, causing you some trouble, bother and aggravation but having minimal repercussions for others. However, sometimes your 'domestic problem' will be thrown in to full view of the general public. Preparing beforehand for the worst can help you limit the damage.

DEALING WITH BIG PR DISASTERS

Small businesses are unlikely to be involved in major incidents or accidents, since they don't own supertankers that can run aground spilling their cargoes; operate Jumbo jets that crash killing hundreds of their customers; or blind thousands of people by releasing toxic chemicals into the air from a plant.

Nonetheless some small businesses can still be prone to accidents, especially if they work in particular sectors. This is especially so if you run a business where you are responsible for the safety and well-being of others. A coach operator with a single vehicle can still have a crash and injure or kill passengers, while a tiny travel agent can still send customers abroad and then find that through lack of funds, or some other reason, it can't bring them back.

Similar things can happen to non-profit organisations – schools who take children on mini-buses, voluntary groups that take children rock climbing or canoeing, sports clubs that arrange trips to football matches and overseas events can all fall victim to bad circumstance. When that happens the press will expect them to have answers to their questions.

THE GOLDEN RULE: BE PREPARED

Try not to wait until something goes wrong before thinking about how you will cope with bad PR should it arrive. The more pre-planning you do beforehand, the more time and effort you will have available to deal with the problem.

Know your local press contacts

Have the names and telephone and fax numbers of your local press contacts written down and readily available. And accumulate basic information about your company or organisation that you can quickly supply to the media.

Write down who will be your local press contacts:

....

....

....

....

Know the people personally

Know the people you will have contact with and talk to if something does go wrong. This could include the emergency services, the general public, relatives and other interested parties.

Write down who these will be:

....

....

....

....

Decide on the spokesperson

Decide who is going to talk to the press about the incident or accident. This needn't necessarily be you. Indeed, if you are apt to feel panicky under pressure then someone else should act as spokesperson. You can always be busy elsewhere trying to resolve the situation. However, on many occasions the press will expect to have their questions answered by the most senior person, not someone else, who could be thought to be shielding them. If you do nominate a spokesperson then explain to the press why they are the most qualified person to do the talking.

Who will talk to the press?

....

Why have you chosen them, or yourself?

....

....

....

....

Imagine some worst case scenarios

Run through all the worst case scenarios you can think of. Have a brain storming session with others if this will help. Don't tell yourself this can't happen or that can't happen. History is full of the 'impossible' occurring.

What are the worst things that can happen?

....

....

....

....

And for each scenario think of what is going to be said; what are the solutions that you can offer; what help can you provide now or how soon can you offer it; how can you improve matters for the future (there may be nothing that you could have done, or do in future to help).

WHEN THE WORST DOES HAPPEN

Understand that when a crisis does occur it is *your* crisis, so make sure you are the one who gets the news out. Don't let someone else beat you to it otherwise when the story does break it will look as though you have had something to hide.

Avoid a cover-up
If you do mess things up so that they affect others, then admit it. If you try to do a cover up, you can be sure that in the short, medium or long run you will be found out and things will be far, far worse. Bad news generally won't lie hidden for long; when it does come out you will be seen not only as incompetent but also as a liar and charlatan. And when these charges are added to your 'crimes', your situation will be worse. Also, you may think that lying to the press is OK, but if the situation becomes serious enough for legal proceedings or similar, how will you be able to cover up then?

If you tell the truth in court (you are in grave danger if you perjure yourself) having previously lied to the press, then you will give them a field day picking over your bones.

Do not alienate the press
Should the crisis be a pure accident over which you have had no control, then don't regard the press with hostility. Supply them with information as quickly and thoroughly as you can. If you don't then they will only start digging. The more that you can organise them, the less they will wander around. It makes sense to let bad news out all in one go. If you release it in dribs and drabs then you will have a series of stories and not just one big headline that is over and done with.

Give the basic facts
Initially, provide the media with basic information about the situation – the how, why, what, where and who of the story. This shows that you are not ignoring the situation and will keep the media somewhat satisfied. Obviously, some facts are sensitive and should be held back. For example, if your company's computer system goes down, then unless a client needs to know about it, keep the information secret. The breakdown could cause people to lose confidence in your company. If you don't want something to appear in the press, tell as few people about it as possible and never mention it off the record to a journalist.

Remember that old chestnut about 'when you are in a hole stop digging'? Well it's absolutely true. Generally any bad PR story will die out sooner rather than later, unless you fan the flames. News is very much of the moment and will remain that way if you let it be. As the days pass, so the story will fade and die a natural death.

If you receive bad press it is often best to let it go, not contradicting, justifying or countering the allegations. Think very carefully about issuing press releases on the subject, especially if they repeat the original story. The press can portray this as 'defending yourself' or 'making claims'. And never let emotion get the better of you. Bite your tongue and hold back.

What to say if confronted

Never speak off the cuff when confronted with a microphone or journalist's notepad. But never say 'no comment' if challenged. Making such a remark allows the press to draw their own conclusions (probably the worst).

Instead of 'no comment', offer the press some form of comment, even if you can't say anything truly enlightening (perhaps you are bound by legal considerations) you can always say that you are in the process of collecting new facts, or that you want to find out exactly what happened before making a statement. This all sounds reasonable and will, 'temporarily' at least, help lift the dreaded press pack off your back.

In a very bad situation, only answer the questions that you are asked. Don't elaborate or expand. Dan Rather, veteran US television reporter, claims there are three responses that you should have when dealing with the press: 'I know and can tell you'; 'I know and I can't tell you'; or 'I don't know'.

When to take legal advice

If in doubt, consult your solicitor about what you can and cannot legally say. Only if you have to, put the solicitor forward as your spokesman. This not only makes it look as though you are hiding, but you consider the situation to be worthy of taking legal advice.

Your right to silence

Ultimately you can always exercise your right not to give an interview or talk to the press. If you are asked to appear on television or radio, but choose not to, then the interviewer can only say that you were asked to appear, they cannot speculate on why you did not accept.

Finally, remember the famous words of Carl Rowan of *The New Yorker*; 'There aren't any embarrassing questions – only embarrassing answers.'

Wrapping up the bad news

If you do have bad news to convey, such as job losses or some other 'negative benefit' try to recover at least some of the lost ground by always looking for the positives in a story.

For instance, you may have to make some people redundant but this means that the jobs of the others are secured; that the company will be in a better position to meet the threat of foreign competition, or that a better service will be provided.

Case history: Simon and Sue face the press

Some unfounded allegations of bad practice are made by a disgruntled ex-client against Simon, an accountant. The local press, with nothing better to do, takes a cursory look at the story with no real thought that anything might come of it.

But when they telephone Simon they're very surprised by his reactions. He is highly defensive about the journalist's questions and offers no information at all to clarify the situation. What's more, he manages to considerably irritate the reporter with his brusque 'no comment' to every question. And though Simon has done nothing wrong, a rather negative story does appear in the press about the dispute, doing nothing for Simon's reputation and temporarily blighting his business.

Sue Hall finds herself in a similar position, but when she is phoned up by the press she adopts the totally opposite tack. Instead of clamming up, she provides them with information. She explains that she is in dispute with the ex-client over a bill and briefly outlines the history of the situation as far as she can without breaching any confidentiality. She states her own position and explains that every business will at some time or another be involved in such a dispute. She says that she has nothing to hide and that she will keep the reporter informed about what is happening.

By now the reporter should be seeing that he doesn't really have much of a story, no more than a petty squabble with a client and that if he makes unfounded allegations, especially if the situation ends up with litigation, he could be storing up trouble for himself. The result, this non-story never sees the light of day.

Appendix
Some Possible PR Ideas

The following ideas are a mixed bag of public relations and publicity ideas. Some of them will be of immediate relevance to you, while others may not be suitable at all, or prohibitively expensive or just too time consuming. Browse and see which you might be able to use, either in their entirety or in part.

Setting up a special interest group

Set up an association that represents your industry or special interest, especially if one doesn't already exist. The benefits are several. First, associations are seen as being independent (even if they are not). This means that they're contacted frequently by the media for comment, views and expert opinion. If you are a spokesperson for the association then your profile is raised and you become an industry expert.

Offering achievement awards

Offer awards at schools and in the community for good sports performances or other achievements. This attaches your name to something worthwhile and creates publicity whenever the trophy is awarded.

Setting up an amenity scheme

Set up a scheme that benefits the community. This might be particularly effective if the local council can't or won't do anything to improve local amenities and the area since this portrays you as the shining white knight coming to the rescue. Good press coverage should result and you also achieve a certain moral standing. Organising the collection of litter in an area of beauty, or inspiring a 'town in bloom' event for the tourist season are examples.

Supporting a special interest group

Provide facilities for a special interest group. Look in the press for groups who are having to give up playing, performing or operating because they don't have the premises, equipment or funding to carry on.

Donating materials to a good cause

Donate materials to a good cause. This in many ways is better than money, since it makes you more involved than just handing over a cheque, which puts an immediate monetary figure on your help. If you are in the trade then handing of over £200 worth of timber for a club house looks more substantial than handing over £200. Having done this don't go overboard in trying to obtain publicity for yourself, it will just look as though you are taking advantage of the situation. Leave others to tell the press how good you are, then you can offer your own low key remarks in response.

Donating funds

Donate funds to a group in need.

Offering advice

Provide free or low cost professional advice to charity and voluntary and non-profit making groups.

Protecting the environment

Protect an animal, plant or creature from local destruction. Is there a national campaign you can tie in with for extra impact? If so, then you might rate a visit from a celebrity.

Nominate a special day

Institute a national or regional day that seeks to promote awareness of a scheme, event, or promotion. Flag Days, Poppy Days, Daffodil Day, are all examples.

Devise a competition

Create a local competition such as 'Superstars event'. Create categories for men, women, boys and girls and senior citizens. Though coverage is mainly local there may be scope for some regional or even national interest. The superstars remain superstars for the year, and are given promotional T-shirts proclaiming the fact and your business name. You could team up with local travel agents and local businesses to offer prizes.

Link up with children or animals

They say never work with children or animals, but involving them can produce good public relations and especially good photo opportunities.

Provide an advice column

Provide an advice and information column for the local newspaper. For instance, a chemist could offer features to the local press on staying fit and healthy while on holiday, the types of proprietary medicines you ought to buy, such as anti-malaria tablets, insect repellent etc.

Offer a special skill

Do you, or anyone else in your company or group, have a special skill that can be exploited, effectively allowing you (or them) to become an expert on the subject? If you can become known as a pundit, then you may be able to earn additional income for yourself, business or group by writing or commenting on your profession, or industry.

Produce a business mini-guide

Write a mini-guide on your subject or area of business and then distribute it to existing or would-be customers. This helps you create a market and positions you as an expert in the field. If you are an accountant you could write and produce a mini-guide on how to set up in business, if you are a security consultant then write one on making your home safe from burglars. Such guides can run from just a few pages to over a hundred. Organisations such as Camra, the AA and RAC are all well known for the publications they produce.

Obtain professional membership

Join a relevant professional organisation. This gives you credibility. If so minded you could eventually become an officer, which creates the opportunity to become a spokesman for the industry (see setting up a special interest group, above).

Smarten up your premises

Make sure the exterior of your premises is in good order. Peeling paint, dead flies in the window and broken panes, hardly make for confidence in your organisation, especially if you are in a sensitive industry that deals with money, health or legal matters.

Attend meetings

Go along or send others along to public and special interest meetings. If you ask questions this will help raise your profile and show that you are involved in the industry or local community.

Syndicate press articles

Syndicate articles about your subject. The same article is offered to many, many different publications who each pay a small fee, perhaps

You will need about 2 hours of studio time to record 30 minutes of tape. The tapes can be sent to clients, industry contacts and even organisers of events and secretaries of associations, if you are looking for speaking engagements.

Produce some video tapes
In much the same way as audio tapes, video tapes can be produced, but make sure they are well put together.

Go 'green'
Link into a 'green' theme. This will make your business more environmentally friendly and generate a caring image.

Link to an educational programme
Connect your cause to an educational programme run by a local school or college. Could you supply equipment, or provide training experience?

Sponsor a minority sport
Sponsoring major or popular sports is hideously expensive, but what about sponsoring minority sports? There will always be opportunities because these activities need money to promote themselves in the early days. Alternatively you could look to the popular sports but sponsor junior, veteran or family events.

Offer free sports facilities
If you run a gym or sports hall, offer free membership to local sportsmen and women who have reached a certain standard.

Promote a friendly rivalry
Manufacture a friendly conflict between yourself and someone else. The rivalry can become more intense, so creating news interest, and then the problem can be resolved, again creating a news story.

Do a joint promotion
Join with another company in a joint promotional venture that publicises you both. You halve costs and can help exploit each others' markets non competitively. Good combinations might be all-terrain vehicles (small personal tractors) and exclusive, quality outdoor clothing; exclusive quality outdoor clothing and shooting courses; suntan lotions and sunglasses; computers and computer books; printing and graphic design services; copywriting and graphic design services. From a public relations point of view, the more unusual the combination the better.

Glossary

Advertising Paid for promotional messages in publications and radio, television and other media.

Advertorial Paid for editorial. You may be asked to supply the copy, but many publications will wish to write it themselves.

Angle The approach used to write a story. Angles are changed to suit particular publications.

Backgrounder Information that supplements a press release.

Brain storming An organised session of creative thinking in which critical analysis of the ideas is left until later.

Breaking stories News that is fresh and developing quickly over a short time. Generally this relates to hard news stories.

Broadsheet A large format daily newspaper, like *The Daily Telegraph* or *The Times*.

Byline The name of the writer or journalist appearing with the feature or news piece they have written. Small news items are generally not bylined, while feature material nearly always is. Those features that are not, are generally written by staff writers in the pay of the publication.

Catchline A descriptive line of copy put on the second and subsequent pages of press release and articles, or on the caption strip of photographs.

Caption Information attached to a photograph or illustration which explains what is happening in the picture.

Column inches the amount of editorial coverage given as measured by the depth of the individual columns of text.

Copyright The legal ownership of a piece of written material or a photograph.

Deep background Similar to off the record.

Doorstepping What journalists do when they turn up uninvited at your office or home, often hanging around for hours. Unlikely to happen unless you are involved in a major news event, often scandalous.

Editorial The words and written copy found in a publication.

Embargo A time and date before which a press release cannot be used.

Exclusive A story that is offered to only one publication.

Feature An article in the press.

Freelancer A journalist, photographer or anyone who is self employed and receives no regular guaranteed salary from an employer.

Freesheets Publications distributed for free, generally locally. They generally contain very much advertising and very little editorial.

Hard news Stories that are generally regarded as being important to the community at large and will be run irrespective of the publication's style and format. Examples of hard news would be disasters, general election results and deaths of VIPs.

Image The perception other people have of you or your organisation.

In-house list A mailing list that is compiled from your own customers, clients and contacts.

Journal A publication, often rather academic in nature and tone.

Layout The design of a document such as a press release, article or newsletter.

Lead time The amount of time, prior to its publication date, that a newspaper or periodical needs all copy.

Leak Information that finds its way to press prematurely. Often this is by accident, but sometimes by design. Leaks are particularly likely to occur when controversial issues and news are involved.

List broker Someone who rents and sells lists of names and addresses.

Locals Newspapers with only local coverage.

Masthead The title of a publication as it appears on the publication complete with logo if applicable.

Media The general term for newspapers, television and radio.

Nationals Newspapers with national coverage.

Not for attribution Information given to a journalist for publication, but with that source of information not to be indicated.

Off the record Information given in confidence to a journalist and not for publication. This should only be done with a journalist you trust highly.

Opinion-former A high profile person who others take note of when forming their own opinions.

Periodical A regularly issued publication, generally a magazine.

Press pack A collection of informative materials including press releases, photos and backgrounders, that are given or sent to journalists.

Press release A sheet or sheets of information sent out to the press.

Proactive PR Where you initiate the story and then maybe wait for others to jump on your bandwagon.

Reactive PR PR done in response to the activities of others and breaking news stories.

Socio-economic groups Groups of people in society, differentiated by job and income.

Soft news Less important news that tends to look at people's life-styles, also includes silly season news. Soft news will be squeezed out by hard news.

Sponsored article An article which is financially supported by a company or organisation outside the publication.

Stringer A local journalist who supplies the national press with local stories, or acts locally on behalf of a national newspaper.

Tabloids Smaller format, popular newspapers such as *Today*, *The Daily Mail* and *The Sun*.

Target audience The people you want to reach and influence with your PR messages.

Top and tail Different beginnings and endings that are added to a standard press release to give it the right angle for a particular publication.

Topspin A new angle given to a story.

Information Sources

PUBLIC RELATIONS

Organisations
Institute of Public Relations, 15 Northburgh Street, London EC1 OPR. Tel: (0171) 253 7020.

Public Relations Consultants Association, Willow House, Willow Place, London SW1P 1JH. Tel: (0171) 222 8866.

Books
ADVANCE – Editorial Features Directory, Themetree Ltd, 2 Prebendal Court, Oxford Road, Aylesbury, Bucks HP19 3EY.

The Artists' and Writers' Handbook (A & C Black).

Benn's Media Directory, Benn's Business Information Services Ltd, PO Box 20, Sovereign Way, Tonbridge, Kent TN9 1RQ.

BRAD, Maclean Hunter Ltd, Maclean Hunter House, Chalk Lane, Cockfosters Road, Barnet, Hertfordshire EN4 0BU.

Creative Review, Centaur Publications Ltd, St Giles House, 50 Poland Street, London W1V 4AX.

Editors (Media Directories) Ltd, 9–10 Great Sutton Street, London EC1V 0BX.

Hollis Press and Public Relations Annual.

Institute of Public Relations Handbook.

The Journalists Handbook, Carrick Media, 2/7 Galt House, 31 Bank Street, Irvine KA12 0LL. Published quarterly and free to selected journalists, otherwise £10. Provides a list of contacts and general background about the press industry.

1000 Markets for Freelance Writers, Robert Palmer (Piatkus).

PIMS UK Media Directory, Pims House, 4 St Johns Place, St John Square, London EC1M 4AH.

PR Planner, Media Publishing Ltd, Hale House, 290–6 Green Lane, London N13 5TP.

Willings Press Guide, Reed Information Services, Windsor House, East Grinstead House, East Grinstead, West Sussex RH19 1XA.

The Writer's Handbook (MacMillan/PEN).

PRESS RELEASES

Software
'Do-it-yourself PR for Business' from CCA Software, Rayner House, 23
   Higher Hill Gate, Stockport, Cheshire SK1 3ER. Tel: (0161) 480
   9811. Price £49 plus VAT.

Books
How to Write a Press Release, Peter Bartram (How To Books, 2nd edition
   1995).

THE PRESS

The National Union of Journalists, 314 Gray's Inn Road, London
   WC1X 8DP (publishes a *Code of Conduct* and *Guidelines for
   Journalists*). Tel: (0171) 278 7916.
Newspaper Publishers Association (NPA), 34 Southwark Bridge Road,
   London SE1 9EU. Tel: (0171) 928 6928.
Periodical Publishers Association (PPA), Imperial House, 15–19
   Kingsway, London WC2B 6UN. Tel: (0171) 379 6268.
Press Complaints Commission, 1 Salisbury Square, London EC4 8AE.
   Tel: (0171) 353 1248.

NEWSLETTERS

Organisations
British Association of Industrial Editors (BAIE), 3 Locks Yard,
   Sevenoaks, Kent TN13 1LT. Tel: (01732) 459331.
British List Brokers Association Ltd, 16 The Pines, Broad Street,
   Guildford, Surrey GU3 3BH. Tel: (01438) 301311.

Books
The Consultant's Guide to Newsletter Profits, Herman R Holtz (Dow-
   Hones-Irwin).
Desktop Publishing Source Book, David Collier & Kay Floyd (Headline).
Graphic Books Catalogue, Graphic Books International, PO Box 3249,
   Lowlands Vale, Guernsey, Channel Islands. Tel: (01481) 48181. Free
   catalogue of graphics and design books.
How to Publish a Newsletter, Graham Jones (How To Books, 2nd edition
   1995).
Marketing and Creative Handbook, Suite 5, 74 Oak Road, Horfield,
   Bristol BS7 8RZ. Lists publicity and marketing support services for
   different areas of the country.

PUBLIC SPEAKING

The Complete Spokesman, Peter Bartram & Colin Coulson-Thomas (Kogan Page).
Dos and Taboos of Public Speaking, Roger, E. Axtett (Wiley).
How to Master Public Speaking, Anne Nicholls (How To Books, 3rd edition 1995).
Janner's Complete Speechmaker, Greville Janner (Business Books).
Just Say a Few Words – The Complete Speaker's Handbook, Bob Monkhouse (Lennard Publishing).
Put it Together, Put it Across, David Bernstein (Cassell).
Speak for Yourself, Richard Denny (Kogan Page).

ARTICLE WRITING

How to Sell Every Magazine Article You Write, Lisa Collier Cool (Writer's Digest Book).
How to Write Articles for Profit and PR, Mel Lewis (Kogan Page).
Put it in Writing, John Whale (Dent).
The Simple Subs Book, Leslie Sellers (Pergamon Press).

CREATIVITY

Use Your Head, Tony Buzan (BBC/Open University).

TELEVISION

BBC Television, Television Centre, Wood Lane, London W12 7RJ. Tel: (0181) 743 8000.
Anglia Television, Anglia House, Norwich, Norfolk NR1 3JG. Tel: (01603) 615151.
Border Television, Television Centre, Durranhill, Carlisle, Cumbria CA1 3NT. Tel: (01228) 25101.
Carlton Television, 101 St Martin's Lane, London WC2N 4AZ. Tel: (0171) 240 4000.
Central Independent Television, Central Broadcasting Limited, Central House, Birmingham B1 2JP. Tel: (0121) 643 9898.
Channel 4, 60 Charlotte Street, London W1P 2AX. Tel: (0171) 631 4444.
GMTV, 5th Floor, The Telvision Centre, Upper Ground, London SE1 9LT. Tel: (0171) 827 7000.
Grampian Television, Queen's Cross, Aberdeen AB9 2XJ. Tel: (01244) 646464.

Granada Television, Granada TV Centre, Quay Street, Manchester M60 9EA. Tel: (0161) 832 7211.

HTV, HTV West, Television Centre, Bath Road, Bristol, Avon BS4 3HG. Tel: (0116) 2778366.

ITN, 200 Gray's Inn Road, London WC1X 8XZ. Tel: (0171) 833 3000.

LWT, London Television Centre, Upper Ground, London SE1 9LT. Tel: (0171) 620 1620.

Meridian Broadcasting, Television Centre, Northam Road, Southampton, Hampshire SO9 5HZ. Tel: (01703) 222555.

Sky Television, 6 Centaurs Business Park, Grant Way, Isleworth, Middlesex TW7 5QD. Tel: (0171) 705 3000.

S4C, Parc Ty Glas, Cardiff CF4 5GG. Tel: (01222) 747444.

Scottish Television, Cowcaddens, Glasgow G2 3PR. Tel: (0141) 332 9999.

Tyne Tees Television, Television Centre, City Road, Newcastle upon Tyne NE1 2AL. Tel: (0191) 261 0181.

Ulster Television, Havelock House, Ormeau Road, Belfast BT7 1EB. Tel: (01232) 328122.

Westcountry Television Ltd, Western Wood Way, Langage Science Park, Plymouth, Devon PL7 5BG. Tel: (01752) 333333.

Yorkshire Television, Television Centre, Leeds, West Yorkshire LS3 1JS. Tel: (0113) 2438283.

Broadcasting standards

The Broadcasting Complaints Commission, 35–37 Grosvenor Gardens, London SW1W 0BS. Tel: (0171) 630 1966.

Broadcasting Standards Council, 5–8 The Sanctuary, London SW1P 3JS. Tel: (0171) 233 0544.

Cable TV Association, 50 Firth Street, London W1V 5TE. Tel: (0171) 437 0549.

Cable Authority, Gillingham House, 38–44 Gillingham Street, London SW1V 1HU. Tel: (0171) 821 6161.

Independent Television Commission (ITC), 70 Brompton Road, London SW3 1EY. Tel: (0171) 584 7011.

RADIO

BBC Radio, Broadcasting House, London W1A 1AA. Tel: (0171) 580 4468.

The Radio Authority, 70 Brompton Road, London SW3 1EY. Tel: (0171) 581 2888.

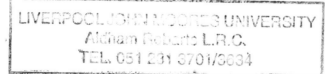

Index